Moments
of Truth

Stories of a Doctor in Subud

RACHMAN MITCHELL

BALBOA.
PRESS

A DIVISION OF HAY HOUSE

Balboa Press books may be ordered through booksellers or by contacting:

Balboa Press
A Division of Hay House
1663 Liberty Drive
Bloomington, IN 47403
www.balboapress.com.au
1 (877) 407-4847

Print information available on the last page.

ISBN: 978-1-5043-1310-0 (sc)
ISBN: 978-1-5043-1311-7 (e)

Balboa Press rev. date: 06/07/2018

"...there is something like a light within the human self that can guide them in accordance with the path for their life."

Muhammad Subuh Sumohadiwidjojo
Susila Budhi Dharma, Kinanti, verse 7.

This book is dedicated to

my Family

my Subud Family

the One Family of Mankind

Contents

Acknowledgements

This series of stories and reflections would not have been published if Maria and Andrew Blake had not read them and felt that others might like to as well. I started out writing my memoirs for myself and my family. It is through their kind encouragement that it has found the light of day for others as well.

However, Maria not only supported me but also edited the book, coordinated the material and liaised with the publisher. She has put in many hours of work.

I thank Hussein Rawlings who encouraged me to write over the years and has worked through the text to suggest edits which give the book greater clarity.

I thank Harris Smart, another Subud brother, who first suggested fifteen years ago I write of my experiences and proposed the title and wrote a book review.

I thank Rohana my dear wife who shared her own recollections of those times and improved the accuracy of my memory of events.

I thank Lorna Dowson-Collins our eldest daughter who for my eightieth birthday present, arranged for various friends to interview me, to get me going on writing my stories.

I thank Isabella Pringle our youngest daughter in helping Rohana in line editing and Davina Pringle my granddaughter in formatting and saving all the stories we thought we had lost!

I thank them all for their generosity of feeling and all their practical help.

It has been a team effort but I take responsibility for the content.

There is some repetition in these stories, which is due to the particular nature and subject that I was writing about. I ask the readers patience for this and for anything they might find offensive or inaccurate.

Introduction

A few years ago, I thought about my grandparent's lives. What did they do? Did they reflect on the purpose and meaning of their lives? Or did they feel these sorts of questions were not appropriate because everything is in the hands of the Almighty, whose purpose for their lives is not to be questioned?

We live in a different very secular era now. I do ask questions, and do not find it is irreverent to do so. In fact, the very opposite.

I then thought of our fifteen grandchildren, and four great grandchildren. Will they ask those same questions I have? And will the stories of my life in which some answers came in the form of experiences, and inner guidance, make any sense to them either now or later?

Life has taught me that the opportunity to get close enough to talk intimately and personally comes only occasionally, and cannot be forced. So, I offer these stories in book or online form in the hope it will stimulate their thinking about the questions we all have in common. And perhaps, God Willing, find some interest or value in seeing how these questions have played out during the course of my life in particular my discovering a Grace called the Subud latihan, and meeting and living with the one who received it first, and through whom it came, Muhammad Subuh.

Preface

The process of learning starts for me by asking questions. Three fundamental questions just dropped into me around the age of 5 years. They were:

Where was I before I was born?
Where will I be after I die?
What lies beyond the blue sky that I am looking at?

Seven years later when I was twelve other questions arose:

What is the purpose and meaning of life?
What is the purpose of my life?

These are questions that many have asked through the generations. They are also the enduring and persistent questions that accompanied my life.

When I was twenty-three something happened, which began the process of answering those questions. I received an experience called the 'latihan', which gave a contact with my soul. While it is difficult to explain what that experience is/was because it exists outside my usual thinking and feeling, it was more real, more natural and normal, and contained an inner dimension and sustenance beyond any experience in my life.

It also involved meeting the bringer of that experience Muhammad Subuh Sumohadiwidjojo whom we came to refer to simply as Bapak (Indonesian for Father, or Respected Elder). Later, after marrying Rohana, we both decided we would like to live near Bapak in Jakarta, Indonesia, with our growing family.

This short book relates stories along the way to getting there, being with Bapak in Indonesia for fifteen years, and then the challenges of adapting to the world again after returning to the West.

I hope it conveys, through certain moments of Truth how I have learnt something of value for myself through following an experience called the "latihan kejiwaan" the training of the soul that is Subud.

Dawn of a New Age

Muhammad Subuh Dawn
and Herald of a New Age

We live in extraordinary times with the pace of change ever accelerating, especially in the fields of science, technology and communication. Our minds are sometimes overwhelmed, and it becomes more and more difficult to be connected to one's Essential Self and through that to All that exists, or as some put it, to God, Allah, Brahma, or whatever language is used to express the inexpressible.

As an adolescent and young man, I could only dimly remember that connection. I say dimly because I had mostly forgotten it, and my conscious, reasoning mind believed that it did not exist. However deep within me was a longing for that connection to come alive again.

The coming of Bapak to Coombe Springs in June 1957 was heralded for me six weeks earlier by an experience which woke me in the middle of the night, and which I now recognise as my opening to the Love and Power of the Almighty. I was suddenly wide-awake and became aware of a ball of bright light above the French doors in front of me. It moved first into my head and then filled the whole of my body, accompanied by an intense blissful happiness, and a feeling of being in my real home. My heart felt itself expanding but it knew it could not expand enough to contain it all. I heard my own voice telling me to follow what the Man from the East had to bring.

A few days later walking along a path I found myself leaping in the air saying "Eureka I have a soul!" I began to become happy. One reason for this was the healing of the grief over my father's death 11 years earlier. I had experienced him sitting beside me, sharing my happiness, while on a train in the London underground.

Bapak Muhammad Subuh Sumohadiwidjojo was the Man from the East that my inner voice had told me was coming. It is astonishing that a human being can have a set of experiences which includes hardly sleeping for a thousand nights, while he is made to move by a Power which he later understands comes from God through his Inner Self. This process continued within him and which he named the latihan kejiwaan (the training of the soul).

That this experience can be handed to others who request it through what we call the 'opening' (a most revealing word), is another extraordinary miracle and is simply told in his autobiography.

Everyone's inner experiences are different according to their individuality born of heredity, culture and much besides. What is more easily recognised in common is what happens to us and the stories we relate to each other; and in the telling and the listening from the heart, we do relate and cheer one another on and up.

Bapak's hopes for us all were expressed in a few simple words "All you need to do now is to put it into practice" and "Everything that you need is there from A to Z" and "The latihan is a continual learning from your Inner Self".

I confess there have been many times when I feel I have disappointed his hopes for us, by not being enough of an example of a true Subud person to attract people to the miracle of the latihan. Thinking and words always get in the way. But when this feeling comes to me, I try to feel what I can do to meet the real need of someone else in some way within my capacity.

Because of the impact this contact with my soul brought, and the experiences of so many of us, I regarded this gift for mankind that Bapak brought as something akin to the return of Jesus Christ. I felt he knew and understood everything, and had power over events, such was the wonderful atmosphere of the miraculous around us. I stood in awe of him. He corrected us, saying he was a fallible man, like us, and that he was no more than a channel for the Power of the Almighty, the Holy Spirit.

Once when he asked forgiveness at the end of a Ramadan and someone said that he did not need to ask our forgiveness, he became quite stern and said he was a human being who made mistakes, and again asked us for forgiveness. This was a great comfort to me.

However, what we witnessed at Coombe, was a man who walked and talked like no other we had ever met. He walked with a visible sense of Presence. When he spoke about spiritual matters there was a man who was talking directly from his experience, rather than talking learnedly about something. His words had a deep ring of truth and made me quiet as they found their mark in my inner feeling. They were such a contrast to the words of the highly charismatic and intelligent Mr Bennett who had held us in thrall for the previous five years. Bapak was always keen to hear our experiences of the proof or benefit of the latihan in our lives.

The latihan has changed my life in many ways: I know now that I have some power of conscious choice. To be miserable and complain about what I don't have, and this list is actually very small, or to be happy and be grateful for what I do have, and this list is very long!

I know also the cause of any insecurity, fear, anxiety or depression in me is quite simply when I lose contact with the Source of my Being in my own soul, which is connected to the source of All Being. It is this which gives my life real direction and real meaning. It is from this I find real love for my family, my friends, community and myself.

3

Muhammad Subuh Sumohadiwijojo (Bapak)

Early Life and the Yearning for Meaning

Rachman 12 months with his father and mother

Dudsland Farm and Frank Clause

I am observing our six-year-old grandson Asoka. He hops, skips and jumps as he walks; his eyes sparkle with joy in the current of life that is running through him. Often, he is on the floor outlining the shapes and colours of the flowers he observes in the garden. He makes collages of stones, shells, and sticks around a jar of water. He has an innate sense of what is beautiful and wants to reflect it - an ancient human need. He says he is not an artist but he is. He pedals his bike around and around our patio letting off high piping sounds of happiness, which in turn makes me happy. He has three older siblings all who care for him and, despite his pranks, openly show their love for him, and of course he has an adoring mother and father.

So! Here is my introduction to my life at his age, as I feel again what it is like to be six years old, although my family relationships were not so secure.

One of the benefits of ageing for me, is that past resentments, grumblings and prejudices gradually drop away and more positive emotions replace them. Especially this is so with my stepfather Frank Harold Clause whom I never really thanked. I was never able to feel close to him the way I was with my father and mother. I realise now that he took on the duties and responsibilities of being a stepfather with great care, discipline and, yes love, which being callow as most youths are, I have never appreciated until now.

He was 49 when he went bankrupt, just at the beginning of the war in 1939. His business had provided him with an upper middle class style of life with seven servants, a large house and gardens, in the 1920s and 30s.

His father, a very successful chemical engineer, had steered him into business. His dream however had always been to live as a simple, self-sufficient farmer producing food for his family and community. He had taken a year off between school and University on a farm in Lancashire, a few years before the First World War. He had fought at Gallipoli in the Horse Artillery becoming a major at an early age. Beside his tall mahogany chest of drawers on which were photographs of his mother, (a Swedish Countess), and his father, hung a picture of Kipling's poem 'IF.' I guess this poem enshrined all the moral values which he tried to adhere to. Once, when I was five, he opened one drawer to reveal a large service revolver. "Not just to shoot the enemy," he said, "but to shoot any who refused to go over the top."

At the same time his business turned to nothing, his marriage to his first wife came to an end with her alcohol addiction and an early death. He met my mother, newly separated from my father, when I was four, and they married when I was five. My sister Sheilagh, myself and Frank's sons Peter and Donald, accompanied them on their honeymoon to a small hotel in Christchurch, a seaside village near Bournemouth.

My mother had just inherited some money from her father who had died two years earlier, and agreed to Frank's wish to buy a 100-acre farm in East Sussex for 2200 pounds.

She prepared me for the move from Northwood Middlesex, by showing me some children's books on farm life and animals which we looked at together. Our reactions to farm life were to be radically different. I loved it and she hated it. She had dreams of being an opera singer, and the opportunity never came again with the restrictions that the farm and wartime life required.

Dudsland farm was a 100-acre farm near Cross in Hand in East Sussex. The farmhouse, about 400 years old, together with the barn, the stables, the cow-house and an oast-house, lay snuggled in a small dip in the landscape. There were then two magnificent beech trees growing adjacent to the back yard of the barn. Nearby was a spring house with a conical roof beneath which lay a limpid, clear, circular pool of spring water, about 3 to 4 metres across. On my first day there, I stood in the shade beside this pool, drinking in the smell of the water and allowing the stillness of the place to wash over me. It was as if Mother Nature had opened both her arms and embraced me. As I explored the farm in those first few days, it was the water and its movement that fascinated me. Animals needed it, plants needed it and, of course, we humans needed it.

Near the gate going into our back garden and orchard was a half-barrel filled by a pipe and overflowing into a stream. It contained a green slime, which I observed as the water flowed through it and past it. The stream, bordered by some small hazel, hawthorn and ash trees, passed through meadows to a wood at the far end of the farm. Here the stream broadened out and flowed over flat stones and over gentle waterfalls. The wood contained mostly chestnut trees with a scattering of oaks, elms and beeches. The movement of the water, the emanations of the trees and the echoing of the bird calls through the wood, always returned me to a state of peace and security within myself, and became my refuge after I heard my mother and stepfather quarrelling.

During that first week, I found the barn which contained a great mound of hay. I climbed to the top and slid to the bottom. After some time, the door into the cow-house opened and an enormously tall man appeared in the doorway. "Aargh aargh git out of here or I'll belt ye", he said. I was sufficiently impressed to obey. But Bailey and his son Ned were to become good friends. Their cottage lay just a few yards from the corner of the '15 acre' and I would spot them loping across the field at the end of work each day. He was immensely strong. He could hold an 8-pound sledgehammer in one hand while hammering the top of a wood pole, which he held in the other hand, an act I have never seen repeated. He was paid the princely sum of five pounds a week. His kitchen garden was well stocked and provided most of their needs. I remember the jam tarts that Mrs Bailey gave me when I made a visit to them.

In the first week, we went to the market at old Heathfield. How many years and centuries had this event been going on every week I wondered? We bought six Light Sussex laying hens and a cock. Our hen house had already been prepared with new, golden yellow chaff from the threshing of the corn spread on the floor. I crawled in through the doorway for the hens, sat in the chaff delighting in the poultry life around me with their clucking and the smell of their warm feathered bodies. I gradually learnt how to take eggs from under a broody hen by holding its neck to stop it pecking me.

The farmhouse had no running water or electricity at first. It was my job to pump 500 pumps of water before going to school, with my butt on one chicken feed bin and my feet on the one opposite.

Going to bed at night, with an oil lamp to guide me up the dark circular stairs to my bedroom, was a little scary. I had very realistic nightmares of heads talking to me from the massive inglenook fireplace below in the sitting room. It seemed as if I was in touch with the people who had lived here in the previous four hundred years.

One day we visited Frank's brother William who was an artist, and had rented a cottage in Rudyard Kipling's estate in Burwash. From there he was painting the wood, which lay below it, which was the inspiration for Kipling to write 'Puck of Pook's Hill'. This is a story of two children meeting people who had lived in the Weald in the past, the first being a Roman legionnaire, another a Norman knight. We bought Kipling's hay mower that was horse driven.

The massive oak beams in our house were said to have been taken from ships that had been sunk, and gave the house a somewhat dark atmosphere. It was the attic that I liked, where the light came in from one end with sunbeams showing up the dust. I could sit there alone and read and imagine what life could be in the future. I read a lot from an early age. I had about 12 volumes of Pictorial Knowledge for Children, those on history, geography, myths and legends being my favourites.

I was intrigued by Plato's story of man never being able to see reality, but only the shadow of it, like a person at the mouth of a cave with his back to the sunlight, only seeing the shadows on the wall in front of him. This impressed me most and still does.

Some mornings I seemed to be easily drawn from my bed to witness the dawn. At those moments every leaf, every twig seemed significant and to awaken me to the intrinsic beauty of everything. Similarly, when snow had fallen and all around was silent and still.

Ah, so beautiful!

Early on, in order to equip the farm, we went to a sale on another farm. The dog there, a beautiful red setter took an interest in me, and I in her. The farmer's wife, noticing this, asked whether I would like to have her and so she came back to Dudsland. With her came her wonderful kennel, big enough for both of us to get inside together, especially when it was raining. She was a wonderful companion to go with on walks around the farm and further. Her life ended suddenly, run over by an army truck at night, and she was buried beside the high stonewall of the cow yard. I grieved for months.

On my sixth birthday, we had a picnic under the enormous oak that grew at the far end of the farm near our small patch of woodland. Our carthorse Jollie was hitched to the 4-wheeled wagon and drew us out there. Donald, my 18-year-old stepbrother, walked out with the jelly. I showed off before my guests, standing on my head.

Frank gave me a small milking bucket with my name painted on it. He also selected two cows, Sooty and Strawberry, chosen for their calm natures, for me to milk when I returned from school each day at 4 pm. I would sit on the metal milking stool with the pail held between my knees, and pull and squeeze on the great teats hanging from the baggy udders of these two cows. I can smell again the fresh warm milk bubbling in the pail, the feel of Sooty's coat against my face, the sounds and the smells of her chewing the cud, and the abdominal rumbling as the grass moved through her intestines.

On my seventh birthday Frank gave me a Welsh pony, Joey, about 12 to 13 hands high, but no saddle. On the first morning, I rode around the orchard area behind the farmhouse and everything was fine until passing through the gate to the muddy road that passed through the farm, his flanks touched the gate post and he bolted. "Hang on to the reins boy!" Frank shouted at me, as I fell off. I obeyed and managed to bring him to a stop, after being dragged 50 yards up the track.

I was to fall off many times, but on grassy meadows, before I finally managed to stay on. Then I was given a cloth saddle. One of Joey's favourite tricks was to gallop full tilt at a gate, and then stop sharply, throwing up his back legs in an attempt to throw me over it. Another time, while bending over in front of him to pick some grass for him, he bit my backside. With his ears back and his eyes rolling it seemed as if he was getting even with me. I rode many miles along the very quiet, country, wartime Sussex roads, whistling or singing songs to him.

I rode him through the lanes to have him shod at the local blacksmith in Hadlow Down. There, I watched as the smithy heated up the horseshoes and shaped them to Joey's hooves, which he had pared before nailing the shoes to them.

In the holidays, it was understood that I did jobs on the farm in the mornings, but was free to play with my friends in the afternoons. One day, I was allowed to go off in the morning. A German plane had been shot down and had crashed into old Heathfield wood. I went with a friend, Peter, and that was my first experience of seeing a dead person. The German pilot's body was slumped over in the cockpit. We collected many bullets from the machine gun belts, and I later withdrew all the cordite for some chemical experiment which I am glad I never went ahead with.

We were dependent on our local tradesmen such as Mr Malpass the butcher, and Mr Herring the baker, who used to come to shoot rabbits on the farm. An invitation to have tea with the Herrings revealed a prized gallstone in a jar on the mantelpiece, testifying not only to Mrs Herring's obesity, but also her capacity to survive a cholecystectomy.

We had to leave Dudsland after three years. Frank had overspent on making the oast-house into a labourer's cottage and the herd had caught TB.

Frank made a move to a smaller farm which just supported us and then semiretired raising chickens. We had three more homes in Sussex but nothing was ever quite like Dudsland.

13

Frank shared his dream with me. There was 45-years difference in age, and I was a boy, and he a man. He was of foreign extraction, wishing to conform to English culture and society, as he saw it, in those days of excessive patriotism in the war. Now, I see that in my adolescent struggle to be free and to be my own self, I could not be near him in my feelings. I wanted to go away, be French, be Russian, be Greek - anything other than a bloody, boring British middle class conformist.

Now I know that I am a British Australian, with Scotland in my blood – carrying so many of their faults and just a few of their virtues. More important is my wish to be a real human being a fellow of All Mankind.

As I stand by his grave with the Norman tower of the parish church rising above me, I look through an arch of hazel and hawthorn over the Sussex fields to the South Downs in the distance. Thank you, Frank, for making possible so many wonderful childhood experiences.

Who Was My Father?

He sits there, his upper face and eyes in shadow from his peaked cap, looking at the photographer, and now me. Quite serious really. His mouth a straight line across his face. Proud perhaps of his survival but aware of the loss of friends and shipmates. Maybe somewhere in his inner subconscious he knows that he will live no longer than a year. His hands are crossed holding his gloves and exposing his three stripes indicating he is a Commander in the Royal Navy. In his mind, this is the greatest institution that has graced this planet. He has survived 6 years in the Arctic and Malta convoys where death by mine, torpedo, dive bomber, or a cruiser shell could have occurred at any time.

I had seen him on short but wonderful holidays with my sister whenever he had some leave. These had been perhaps only four in all through the six years of the war. On one of them he had asked me, "How would you deal with a man running at you with a knife to stab you?" As I acted the part of the man running at him he quickly flipped me over his shoulder in a nice jujitsu move.

My first memory of him was on the back of an elephant in a sunny glade in the Indian jungle where he worked in the Forestry service. I was less than three years old when my mother left him for his infidelity. Deep within both myself and my sister was the knowledge that we had a father who loved and cared for us despite the breakup with our mother.

The photo I am looking at was taken a day before we last met up, on my twelfth birthday at the Cumberland hotel opposite Hyde Park in London. I asked him why he was bald and he told me his hair had all fallen out at the Battle of Jutland in the First World War. He was a young midshipman on the Warspite when the ship was hit by many enemy shells at the same time. As I talked with him I had no idea what it would be like to be in a huge battleship, with sides that were 7 inches thick to repel the huge shells that were fired some 12 kilometres away, and the racket and sense of acute fear that the crew would have felt.

I only wanted to know "Who won?" My father said "We did." In fact, it was inconclusive. The Royal Navy suffered more loss of ships and men. The German navy withdrew to the Baltic and never came out again. That is, all except their submarines which did devastating damage to Allied shipping.

There were 300-midshipmen on the Warspite, one of them being Mountbatten - his name comes just a few lines below my father's name in the Navy lists of midshipmen at the time. Its chaplain was Walter Carey, an Oxford Blue in boxing and rugby, who later became our school chaplain at Eastbourne College[1]. He was a hero in the battle, dragging burning sailors out of blazing gun turrets that had taken a hit. My father remembered him well with respect and affection and wrote to him once after the war.

I was proud of my father and his warrior past. He bought me a board game called Dover Patrol which was really a replay of the battle with the relative strengths of battleships, battle cruisers, destroyers, minesweepers and submarines.

---

[1] See 'Bishop Walter Carey'

Why was I not curious to know more? Well, as I survey my grandchildren I see they have little curiosity about what happened in my life. They naturally want to get on and live theirs.

Over the course of my life my loyalties have changed. Loyalty to the Royal Navy, loyalty to the British Empire, and loyalty to the Sovereign of Britain are all now superseded by a loyalty to the idea, the concept, the understanding of One Mankind, inspired by Bapak who regarded humanity as one, and who constantly reminded us of that.

Rachman's father Commander J.E.M. Mitchell

Bishop Walter Carey

"Are you midshipman Mitchell's son?"

The question seemed to me, at the tender age of twelve, to be clear evidence of some extrasensory, intuitive, spiritual attribute of the questioner, who was Bishop Walter Carey. I had no idea how he knew.

He was taking a scripture class in 1945 at Ascham St Vincent's, the Prep School for Eastbourne College, and asking everyone their names. At that moment, I did not know he had been chaplain on board HMS Warspite during the Battle of Jutland, together with my father who was then 19 years old. Those present at that terrible battle had a sense of comradeship with everyone else on that ship for the rest of their lives.

I realised later my father had recognised Bishop Walter Carey's name in the school book, and had written to him.

He came to Gonville House where the Prep school started, with a dozen boarders, before Ascham house was ready. What was clear to me from the time I first saw him was his enthusiasm for life which seemed connected to his belief in the teaching and example of Jesus Christ. His formation as a man was in the Edwardian era, and included the moral principles of the Evangelical movement, as typified by Lord Shaftesbury. In his retirement, he planned to tour England in his old Austin Seven and preach the Gospel in all its villages. I remember him standing in the College chapel pulpit, his arms outstretched to us. "Boys, boys! Without Christ, you are lost", or as he pronounced it "l o r s t".

He was a great believer in sport as a facilitator for moral principles of courage and fighting spirit. I remember him at the side of the boxing ring at Ascham cheering on both myself and my opponent Kelly. It was a draw but I had had a battering and the next time I boxed Kelly, I lost.

The problem for me were the questions that I was asking myself. I was a star gazer and a reader of Jeans and Eddington, the astrophysicists of that time, whose writing gave a sense of the enormous size of the Universe. I had always sensed its vastness as I gazed out on a clear night. How could the Creator of All That have a son, a human son?

At the time, allegory and symbols were not part of my understanding, and the subjects of Science and Religion were in collision in my mind. One appealed to my rational mind, the other to a yearning for spiritual guidance. It took many years for an understanding to come to me, when my heart and mind could become still and silent, and able to receive what I needed to receive. Indeed, now I know that the seven beatitudes of the Sermon on the Mount are the essence of a truly happy life.

Bishop Carey, with his connection to my father, his sincere and enthusiastic faith, his courage and robust masculinity, was an important figure in my early life. I have my little Book of Common Prayer signed by Walter Carey with "good luck" written in Greek in it, and give thanks in my heart for his influence on me.

The Old Lady Who Speaks to Me

I am twelve years old again, on holiday in Edinburgh, the childhood home of both my parents. In fact, I am on Princes Street just near where my maternal grandfather had his business, and the street along which he used to walk to his church. He was a close friend of the Minister and indeed was an Elder of this Church, St George's. My parents were married here.

I am idly gazing in a window when an old lady approaches me. "Whatever happens to you believe in the Lord," she says.

I am embarrassed. I do not like religion being preached to me in the streets. However, she is kindly, looks me in the eyes and then moves off.

Now 70 years later I cannot think of a better piece of advice to base one's life on, although maybe what she meant by "Believe in the Lord" is slightly different to what I understand it means.

Two days later I am staying with my Aunt Rena in Pitlochry in the Highlands. The cooking smells permeate the home of this kind woman. I am in the large hallway of her bungalow where I had lived seven years earlier in the war, when we were evacuated to Scotland. She is in the bathroom and I hear her sobbing and wonder why.

She has been reading a telegram from my stepmother in India, which states that my father has died after a fall. She liked my father and had been a bridesmaid at my parent's wedding, but she is crying for me also. In those early days, we were a close family.

My sister has just passed her physiotherapy exams and is about to fly out to India as a congratulatory present. Her grief is just as great as mine, maybe more. I feel an awful emptiness inside me. Where has he gone? No! He is not really dead; it is all a mistake, a bad dream. He will suddenly turn up one day.

I do not think I cried much, my feelings seemed anaesthetised. I did not want to recognise the truth and so for many a year it remained buried. I was unable to enjoy life with the same humour and social engagement that he did. I clung to the memories of the time we spent together, when he was on leave during the war. He showed his love and care by always visiting us and enjoying our company.

To this day, I look at his photograph now standing on the piano in my study and feel the love of a son for his father. The healing came in a most unexpected way eleven years later.[2]

---

[2] See the story 'My Opening in Subud'

Rowing

One can either row alone or in pairs, fours or eights. Most of my experience with rowing from the age of 15 to 18 was in 'fours'. It was great, firstly just for the strengthening of one's body and seeing what it is capable of. Secondly, and not necessarily in that order, was the experience of being part of a crew who are all dependent on one another. In addition, there was the role of 'stroke', which teaches self-reliance. All of this develops self-confidence from seeing the results of one's efforts. It also gave me a position in school society, something necessary for me who was, and still is, a bit of a dreamer.

However, there is something else which occurred once or twice which I can only describe as a quite heavenly feeling, when a certain perfection is reached with all four men in the boat. The balance of the boat, the rhythm, and the rate are all just right. We are all together in perfect unison. Wow!

We had come to Eton in the Easter of 1951 to train for the Marlowe Regatta the following June. We stayed in a small guesthouse in the village of Eton and borrowed our boat from the Eton boat club. We asked the old guy who looked after the boat shed how much we should pay and were told that rowing is not to be paid for with "filthy lucre".

I took the bus from our home in Sussex, a long trip complicated by the fact that I had a burning hole in my foot. The cause of this pain was our school doctor, a retired Royal Navy surgeon captain who was probably a little addicted to the bottle. His first attempt to remove a verruca from my foot had occasioned a flourish of his scalpel, resulting in an unnecessary slash in my foot. His next attempt to remove it was by caustics, which he failed to tell me how to use, hence the burning hole in my foot.

This experience of pain on that bus trip led to determined efforts to lift my consciousness, by directing my attention in order to minimise the pain. I attended the Eton school doctor, whose careful attention to the wound and general sympathy with my situation was one of the factors that led me eventually to become a doctor myself.

I can remember most of the names and personalities of the rowing crew. Berry Parlett was captain and also head prefect of our house. He went on to be Professor of Mathematics at University of California, Berkeley. There was also Guy Landon and Michael Noble and our diminutive Cox, whose name I cannot remember.

We had long rows right up to Maidenhead and back. We were building stamina, strength and coordination and I was testing myself as 'stroke', deciding when to raise the rate and when to settle into a steady pull. That area of the Thames has meadows beside it and trees, which sometimes reach over the water to provide shade.

Marlowe Regatta happened just after the weekend at Oxford University in which I took my entrance exam. My talent for rowing helped. So, did the fact that my housemaster, William Betts, had been a colleague in the War with the Provost of Worcester College, a man called Masterman. They had worked together to break the Nazi naval code. These were the factors that, in those days, influenced success or not in gaining entrance to an Oxford College. I had stayed in the De Quincy room where, a hundred years earlier, De Quincy had smoked opium and had written down his experiences in a well-known book 'Confessions of an English Opium Eater.' It was a fantastic summer weekend, looking over the courtyard and dining in the hall of a College I would never attend. Although I was accepted to study History, I later changed my mind and decided on medicine.

When the day for the Marlow Regatta arrived, we were issued with a boat in which the outrigger to my oar was faulty, so that unless the balance of the boat was perfect, I could not get my "hands away" which is vital. We lost, but our defeat was mollified by a splendid meal at the Compleat Angler hosted by Berry Parlett's parents. They later invited me to stay with them and gave me my first contacts with the Work of Gurdjieff which in turn lead to my life-long spiritual path, the Subud latihan.

Beresford Parlett and the Work

June the 9th 2014. I was due to meet an old-school friend, Berry Parlett, in the waiting room of Brighton station at 11 am. We last met some 62 years earlier, and I wanted to see the person who had played a role in setting the direction that my life was to take. He had not received the email telling him that I was still in Australia in hospital with a broken hip and cardiac arrhythmia. But we have been in contact again and met up finally in 2015.

We had each been members of the school's rowing and fencing teams. He, being a year or two older, was the captain of both. More importantly we were both members of the philosophy club run by an enthusiastic Math's tutor. Thus, we had discussed together many of the great philosophical questions of life.

From the age of thirteen onwards there was only one question that really mattered to me. "What is the meaning of life in general and mine in particular?" Books on Freud, Buddhism, the Upanishads, Henri Bergson, Plato, the Greek myths - I read them all but no answer was really coming to me. Then Berry handed me a book called 'In Search of the Miraculous' by Peter Ouspensky. The book is an account of the meetings in 1913 between the Russian author Ouspensky, a renowned journalist and mathematician of that time, with Mr G.I. Gurdjieff, a Greek Armenian philosopher.

I let go of the book a long time ago as life took a different turn for me, but recently I downloaded it from the net and it had the same startling effect on me as it did 63 years ago. Like a dash of cold water.

Man is asleep.

Governed by forces that he is unaware of, he sleepwalks through life.

Only by intense work on himself by self-observation can he prove for himself this truth, and only by intense commitment can he free himself from slavery to these unconscious forces that act on him all the time.

He cannot remember himself for long, however hard he tries.

His different centres of thought, feeling and movement are uncoordinated and often at odds with one another.

Gurdjieff did not ask that you believe him. He just said, 'Observe yourself and see what conclusions you come to'. However, there was a hitch. In order to work on yourself you needed help. You needed a teacher. As an impressionable sixteen-year-old, I swallowed it whole. The burp was not to come for another seven years. Gurdjieff's ideas were sometimes called the 'Work' and sometimes the 'System'.

I met Berry's parents for the first time when we lost our rowing race at Marlowe regatta and they took us all to the Compleat Angler, a lovely old world pub, to have a consolation meal. When Mrs Parlett who was a follower of the Work, heard of my interest in the ideas of Gurdjieff she invited me to stay a weekend with them in their Chelsea flat. She gave me introductions to leaders in the Work in the US where I was about to go for an English-Speaking Union scholarship. These included John Sinclair, Second Baron Pentland, who was CEO of a small company which did aerial oil exploration, and Dr Walsh who had attended Gurdjieff in his last illness, two years earlier in Paris.

I stayed in New York for a week with a friend of my mother's who had an apartment on the corner of 57th Street and 7th Avenue. During that time, I phoned Lord Pentland and had an immediate invitation to meet him at his office. His generosity took me by surprise. Here was someone who had achieved a first-class honours degree in Science at Cambridge and had inherited a Scottish title and a seat in the House of Lords. He had been placed in charge of all the 'Work' groups in the US ahead of older and more experienced people in the 'Work' - and me just an exchange scholar.

He gave me the address of an old personal friend (not in the Work) who lived in the small town of Washington, Connecticut, where the school I was studying at was located. He also gave me contacts in Princeton which I intended to visit in the Easter holidays, in particular to see Dr Walsh, the doctor who had looked after Gurdjieff in his last illness. He invited me to stay with him and his wife in his holiday cottage on Coney Island. I only realise now, as I am writing, that his kindness and attention may have arisen because of Berry Parlett's mother, who could well have written to him about me.

I visited Dr Walsh in the Easter holidays, staying with a senior academic of the University whose house was very near to that of Einstein. I was suffering at that time a common symptom of adolescence, postural hypotension, that is, every time I stood up quickly, I would feel a little faint and giddy. Dr Walsh listened and then examined me and did an ECG, and took my blood pressure sitting, lying and standing. His manner and his method impressed me. I had already come to the conclusion that my chief interests in life were people and science and therefore, medicine was the field I should work in.

It happened a house guest, who was staying at the same time I visited, was the daughter of Kenneth Walker, a successful surgeon. He was the author of a number of books including 'Venture with

Ideas', an account of his meetings with Gurdjieff and of the ideas of the Work. She gave me their address in London and her father's phone number.

It was this visit that really crystallised my wish to follow medicine as a career. How I eventually managed it is another story. It was Kenneth Walker's advice to me, to give up my place at Oxford to study history and instead, start at the bottom again to get four science A levels (the first MB) and then to apply to different medical schools. All these memories and thoughts were going through my head when Beresford (as he is now called) and I eventually met up two years ago at East Grinstead railway station, to spend a day together.

This had been preceded by an exchange of emails over about 9 years. After winning an open scholarship to Oxford, reading Maths for his B.A. and working in his father's timber agents firm for three years, he emigrated to the States. He earned a Ph.D. in Maths at Stanford University and eventually became a professor at the University of California, Berkeley. He published a monograph on the computation of matrix eigenvalues.

He and his wife joined the Work group in San Francisco in 1960. After 20 years, he felt a sharp drop in his spirits every time he entered the house where meetings were held. After a year of this feeling he felt a hand on his back pushing him away and he dropped out of the Work. He has dabbled in Zen but his energy now goes to research in Maths.

He reminded me that I had smuggled him in to the large hall at Coombe Springs, called the Djamichunatra, when Bapak came to England and gave his first talks.

Beresford felt very grateful for his education at Eastbourne College, and sent his son from the US to study there for a year. At first I did not find this gratefulness arising within me. However, over time I began to understand that my unhappiness at school was due to grieving over my father's death and my inability to talk about it. Looking back, I realise I received many kindnesses at Eastbourne.

When we met in 2015 we shared a meal together with our wives. He then came down to spend a day with me in our farm stay lodging in the Ashdown Forest in Sussex. It was so easy to speak to one another and exchange our life stories.

He was now a much less competitive person than when I had known him at school; having achieved a lot in his field of mathematics and taught at the University of California, Berkeley he had no need to prove himself. However, I felt intuitively that certain experiences of loss had refined his character resulting in a naturalness and humility that I had not been aware of before.

The Coming of
the Latihan

My Opening in Subud

It was 1957 and I was a member of the young persons' group in the Gurdjieff Work led by JG Bennett. I was living at Coombe Springs as a medical student and partook in the very active community life there. My main duties were washing up, serving tables and helping keep the large garden beautiful. In addition, I was also helping to build a seven-sided building to hold our meetings.

Bennett had been opened in Subud almost a year, together with six of his students whom he had selected to experience and assess the latihan. At the same time, he was carrying on the Work groups that had been going on for some time which focused on self-observation and the various exercises that we were given to facilitate this process.

The young people's group met every morning at 7am in his study on the first floor of the building. Often in the winter months there would be a fire crackling in the fireplace and he gave us exercises to sharpen our senses. For instance, to listen to all the different sounds that the fire made. This was always preceded by a period of active relaxation when we let go and sensed our bodies, starting with the muscles of the face then to the shoulders and arms then to the hips, legs and feet etc. It was and still is a useful exercise to be more aware and less driven by our thoughts.

The stream of different visitors that now came to Coombe alerted us to the possibility that something new was about to happen. Then one morning Bennett said to us all, "Someone is coming from the East who will alter the direction of our work."

Actually I did not think much about this. I had no idea what it meant.

However, a few nights later I suddenly awoke, in a state of alertness never experienced before. I saw a ball of light above the French-window, it moved into my head and then down into the whole of my body and I was filled with a feeling of joy and bliss. In fact, my heart was bursting, unable to take it all in. I heard my own voice guiding me to follow what the man from the East had to bring. I felt as though I had returned to my true home. Then I fell asleep.

The next days were normal days of up and down but one day I was walking down a path to a building called the "fishbowl" (because it had so many windows) and spontaneously I was jumping in the air and saying "Eureka, I have a soul!"

My father had died some ten years earlier, when I was twelve. I had never adequately dealt with the grief and issues surrounding his death. The question, "Where has he gone?" still troubled me. Despite a fair success at school I did not feel close to anyone and was unable to communicate my feelings of loss and loneliness, instead I had a tendency to self-pity and I took refuge in reading and philosophy. I experienced an anaesthesia of my feelings, and a sense of detachment between mind and feeling.

Shortly after the experience of the ball of light, I was travelling in a London underground train when I felt my father sitting beside me. It seemed that not only did I have a soul, but he also had one. I understood that the soul was the central part of me that linked me not only to my family but to Everything. Hence there was no need for me to continue in my sadness. It was an enormous relief! I no longer felt lonely and isolated in life. In fact, for the first time I began to feel very happy.

Was this just spiritual euphoria? How much self-deception was going on? What was happening to me was causing me to feel light and clean as if a burden was lifting off me. It felt as if both my spirit and my body were being cleansed. That the latihan was a cleansing process was what 'the man from the East', whom we came to call Bapak, later explained to us. To some people, it may have seemed that we were susceptible to suggestion or perhaps being hypnotised. But for me, the proof of the pudding was in the eating of it.

My self-awareness and self-confidence increased. What is strange is the process of Self Observation, which in the "Work" demanded effort, intention and will, now flowed naturally and spontaneously by itself.

The experience of the ball of light happened about 6 or 7 weeks before I was officially opened. We all trooped into the dining room at Coombe with really very little explanation at all. We were asked to stand up, believe in the Power of God and surrender ourselves to it. Someone then said "Allahu Akbar" and walked around the room saying that. We all had our eyes closed and I ended up on the floor not knowing really what had happened to me, except that whatever it was, it was good and right.

I cannot remember whether I went to Scotland to stay at my Aunt Edith's hotel outside Aberfeldy before or after my official opening. There I climbed Ben Laws and experienced a heightening of my senses and intense joy and energy.[3]

There were many similar stories of those early days of Subud, with incidents of sudden loud explosions of joy and energy. I witnessed

---

[3] See 'The Heart of the Highlands'.

the racket in the large chicken houses - temporary structures that were hired to provide space for latihan on the lower lawn of Coombe Springs. There could be 4 to 5 sessions in an evening and the movement could be quite violent. This included people going through windows, rolling out of the door in a carpet, and rapid stamping on the floor so that it reverberated like a bad musical instrument. Throughout all this Bapak remained calm and when he walked, his walk was light and alive. This was an example of the process of the latihan in himself, and it was an encouragement for others.

My life began to change. I ceased my reading of esoteric spiritual literature and began to pay more attention to my medical studies with the aim of becoming a practical and effective physician.

The Heart of the Highlands

It was a steep climb but I was fit, reasonably so for a twenty-three-year-old medical student. Ben Laws is one of the Munros, or Highland mountains of over 3000 feet. I was going to say 'hills', but people have died on those hills in snow storms. However, this was April and the sun was shining.

I stood at the top, looking over my beloved Scottish Highlands, my ancestral home, though little more than a year of my life had been spent there.

There was Loch Tay below me with the sun shimmering on its surface and further in the distance Loch Rannoch. I could see all around for miles. Suddenly I became still inside, nothing forced, it came by itself. I was used to finding great landscapes inducing a state of quiet contemplation in me, but this time it was different.

Spontaneously my arms came up by themselves and I began to turn like a Mevlevi Dervish, singing and shouting I know not what, at the top of my voice. It was a state of exhilaration and exaltation in the very essence of Life within me, which I had not known quite like this before. The usual burble of my head had gone, instead my senses were alive. Every sound and smell and sight were sharpened, and indeed 'made sense'. My body was suddenly filled with enormous energy, and I was running and leaping like a stag along the ridge of the mountain and then slithering down its slope. There was a pool in the stream pouring over the rocks with a dead sheep stuck just a few metres down. I stripped as the sweat was pouring off me, even in this cool spring air, and bathed in the icy water. I did not rest when I was dressed again but half walked, half skipped with this energy and feeling of happiness still bubbling through me.

When I passed through Glen Lyons, the sounds of bleating lambs filled my ears and the subtle mauves of the heather delighted my eyes. I passed only one place of habitation on my way back. This was a shepherd's croft, a low, thick, stoned-walled dwelling, whitewashed on the outside. I knocked on the door and asked the owner for a glass of water. As I sat in the semidarkness, he continued making his porridge, stirring real oats gradually into the boiling water - no ersatz Quick Quaker Oats here! There was no need for conversation, both of us were happy in our own worlds.

I was back at Edith's Hotel at Coshieville before sunset, a little tired and foot sore after a walk of 18 miles. Slowly my normal state returned, after this brief experience of one kind of heaven.

Meeting Rohana

Gratitude has been a long time arising in me, and now as we celebrate together our fiftieth wedding anniversary, I feel unbounded thankfulness to the One who brought us together. This union has also been the origin of our children, grandchildren and great grandchildren and for this my gratitude knows no bounds.

In particular, there are five people that I thank who, although no longer present on this Earth, made our union possible.

It was 1955 and Rohana was sweet seventeen, just down from school and I was a twenty-one-year-old medical student. The place was a large Edwardian mansion called Coombe Springs. The exact spot was in the entrance hall where she was looking at the notice board in a disinterested way. She was beautifully, neatly, but simply dressed. As now, clothes well chosen, say something of the order of her character. She was like a breath of fresh air.

I had entered by the large front doors and my reaction on seeing her was unusual for me at that time. I lived a disciplined, serious life in the pursuit of work on my Self, something that could and did lead to self-obsession and taking myself far too seriously. I retreated out of the doorway and began to run around the lawns and rose garden shouting, "Hooray!" I had no idea that six years later we would become man and wife. I was only partly aware this 'breath of fresh air' would be part of the wind that would blow some of the cobwebs out of my mind.

Here is the chain of events that lead to our meeting and marriage.

As related earlier, through Mrs Parlett, the mother of a school friend, I had become a follower of Gurdjieff's work, led by John Bennet at Coombe Springs. Although the ideas of 'The Work' are indeed true, the methods to free one's self from the influences which prevent the development of the soul, or essence of a person, were too difficult for me. Indeed, it appears it was like that for many who lived and worked there. We became rather humourless and heavy, at least that is how I now see myself at that age.

For a while, John Bennett had realised this too. When he heard of Subud, he and six of his students were opened and followed the 'latihan' of Subud. After they became convinced of its benefit, they invited its founder, Pak Subuh or 'Bapak', to come to Coombe Springs. He was the first to receive this latihan, its meaning and benefit, both for himself and the rest of mankind. The effect of the latihan on me was to make me a happier person who could actively enjoy life. It gave me enthusiasm to follow my chosen career as a doctor. It also caused the arising in me of the wish to get married and have a family.

Rohana's mother, Dodie, was in my Gurdjieff group that met at Coombe Springs every second Saturday. We were set various tasks to do in the intervening time and would report back on our observations. Dodie had a lot of faith in Mr Bennett and the ideas of 'The Work' so she, like many of us, followed his suggestion to be 'opened' to receiving the latihan of Subud.

It happened at that time that a famous actress, Eva Bartok, became ill with an ovarian tumour while pregnant. She had been a Gurdjieff student under John Bennett for some time, and had readily followed his suggestion to be opened. She asked Bennett whether she should have an operation on the tumour. He then asked Bapak, whose advice was not to have the operation which might harm the pregnancy, but to fully surrender herself to the Power of Almighty God. Both Bapak and his wife accompanied Eva Bartok in her latihan. After a few weeks the tumour had disappeared and her pregnancy progressed normally.

This brought Subud into the news and many people came flocking to Coombe in search of a cure for their ailments. Bapak was clear that the aim of the latihan was towards a person's true worship of God and for the development of one's self to become a realised human being. However, if in the process someone was cured, then that was a sign of God's mercy.

A number of the financial supporters of Coombe Springs got together under Bennett's guidance and bought a property called Brookhurst Grange in the Surrey countryside. This was to be a Nursing home, where the latihan augmented the normal medical practice. A number of staff following the latihan were recruited to run the place and Lavinia (formerly Dodie) became resident matron with a staff of about six nurses. Helpers came down from Coombe Springs to do latihan with the patients and the staff also followed their own latihan. Medical care was carried out by an excellent GP called Kevin Browne.

I looked for my first job as a doctor to be as near Brookhurst Grange as possible, because I wished to observe and witness what was happening. Rohana had joined her mother when Lavinia lived at Coombe Springs, and now Rohana came to Brookhurst in her holidays. That is where we started to go out with each other.

So, on this path which led eventually to our marriage, I find the feeling of gratitude for my good fortune goes first to Bapak for bringing the latihan, this contact with the Power of Almighty God. For that, I will be forever grateful.

Then there is the kindness of Mrs Parlett, my friend's mother who introduced me to John Bennett.

Then to John himself, who would later lose faith in the latihan which he brought to so many of his fellow humans. I still cannot thank him enough for being the means to my own journey in Subud.

Next, there is my mother who approved of Rohana both inwardly, when she advised me in a dream,[4] and outwardly, when she approved of our intended marriage.

Finally to Lavinia, Rohana's mother who followed first the Gurdjieff Work, then the latihan and brought her daughter into my life

---

[4] See story Marriage Guidance

Marriage Guidance

"What is a 12 letter word for lucky?" she asked, while sipping her morning cup of tea in bed.

"Providential", he said, the word seeming to come from nowhere. He looked across at her as a wave of gratitude and love passed through him.

"Yes", he said to himself, "I have been lucky and Providence has provided me with the right woman to be my wife".

That inner certainty had not always been there and he casts his mind back fifty-four years when he was so uncertain and so muddled.

He, once again, is in the room he had as a young house surgeon at Redhill County Hospital. The young residents lived in an old Victorian house just 100 yards from the hospital. They were on 36 hours at a time, often exhausted from calls at night to attend emergencies. He felt relief at being at last able to apply the skills that had been learnt over six years of study at medical school. However, he could not relax until he had dealt with another unmet need, that of getting married.

He had found someone and they felt drawn to one another. They also annoyed the hell out of one another and their characters were like chalk and cheese.

He liked to see life in general in a broad sense, she liked to be specific and to the point. Honesty and integrity were (and are) her hallmarks, along with down-to-earth practicality. He liked to wander off in his mind and consider everything through a philosophical lens and always try to see both sides of a question.

They would discuss history. She had set out in medical school at the Royal Free and had changed to the study of history. He had had a place at Oxford to study history and had changed to medicine. She had bought my half skeleton from me when she began her study of anatomy. Her historical heroine was Elizabeth the First. "Cruel scheming vixen," said he, "Mary Queen of Scots had a heart and provided Britain with a King who sponsored the translation of the Bible into English. That changed not only Britain, but the world." The arguments were intense enough to ask himself if they should marry.

For him the seriousness of the question was affected by the fact that his parents had split up four years after he was born. He loved both of them with equal intensity and suffered their separation deeply. It was as if his own self had been split and thus he needed guidance from beyond his own limited wisdom.

He was considering this one evening, as the sounds of lovemaking from the next room, between the prim faced theatre sister and the lusty Anaesthetics Registrar, were coming through the wall. It made him more aware of the unmet needs of his own body. They were to be met, according to his conscience, only within the bond of marriage. He knew, however, that the choice of a wife was better not met via the smouldering come hither glances of sensual women, nor indeed, by the stirring of romantic feeling which he had felt for a widow ten years older than himself with six children.

There was another question. Where was he going to find the money for an engagement ring that would cost a fifth of his meagre yearly salary? Pondering these thoughts and feelings, he went into a very deep sleep and had a dream, a clear dream he would remember for the rest of his life.

He found himself on the top of a church where his parents had married thirty-eight years earlier in Edinburgh. He looked across the lead lined roof and saw his mother who wanted to give him some advice. "If you want an engagement ring for your fiancée, go to the jewellers to the King," she said. He woke the next morning refreshed but uncertain of the meaning of the dream.

Two weeks later he went down to see his mother at her country cottage in Sussex. He asked her for a loan to buy an engagement ring. She replied that she would willingly lend him the money, but she had a ring which her mother had given her, and if he liked it, he could have it.

The ring was a blue sapphire surrounded by twelve small diamonds. It sat in a box on the lid of which was inscribed, 'So and So Jewellers to King James VI' - of Scotland.

He recalled his dream and was struck by the coincidence. It was clear his mother not only approved of Denia (later Rohana), but the dream and her actions reflected the rightness of this choice. They were married in the church where her parents had married and which Denia had attended as a child.

Back to the present.

"How did you get that word providential? I would never have thought of it," she said.

"By good luck and the insight and intuition of a good mother," he thought.

Rachman and Rohana Mitchell's wedding

Wedding Ring - Lost and Found

A few months after our honeymoon Rohana and I went to bathe in a lake near Guildford. I love swimming in any kind of water but Rohana is not so fond of swimming.

I was already in the water and saw her sitting on the edge of the bank and waded over to her saying "Come on in, Darling". I put my hands up around her upper arms to pull her into the water. My hand passed over her fingers and the wedding ring spun into the lake.

We dived and dived and could not find it. My heart got heavier each dive, as I felt guilty about forcing her in rather than taking her own time. It seemed an awful omen.

I spoke about it with a close friend, Norman Kermode, who said "Don't worry, I have goggles and I love to dive." The next weekend we went to the spot and we saw the gold ring glittering in the sunlight through the water on the bottom of the lake.

Thank you Norman. Sadly, he remained single for the rest of his life.

Now as I look back on a long and fruitful marriage, I realise that I have been truly lucky that Providence has provided me with such a worthy and lovely woman.

The Coffee Pot

The morning sunlight is flickering through the trees edging the little river Crane that meanders around the common lawn of our block of flats in Twickenham. We are very happy, Rohana and myself, just beginning our third year of marriage. I am seated opposite Martin, then eighteen months old and seated in his baby chair, looking out on this peaceful scene, having breakfast together.

A large pot of coffee stands on the oak gate leg table surface and Rohana comes in and sits down. We begin a discussion that turns into an argument as she is in a hurry to prepare for Martin's Christening that day and I wanted my lazy Sunday morning breakfast.

I am continually surprised, by the passions this little woman arouses in me; I was so peaceful, quiet and centred as a bachelor! And here I am, suddenly shouting "No, no I just can't take this!" To emphasise my frustration, I lift the coffee pot and bring it crashing down on to the table. The coffee shoots out and hits the ceiling and spreads everywhere and I am shamefacedly trying to clear the resulting mess up, while Rohana tries to get the coffee off the ceiling.

About a month later we are again having breakfast together, with Martin seated in his baby chair, and again we are beginning to get into an argument. Suddenly we notice our son jumping up and down in his chair pointing to the ceiling, which still has a very faint coffee stain on it. This time we collapse with laughter.

Forty-eight years later Martin phones me on a regular basis from New Zealand, pointing out and suggesting more creative ways of behaviour. It is much appreciated.

Bapak's First Visit to Scotland

When I heard that Bapak had been invited to Scotland to open new people, I wanted to be there to witness the start of Subud in my native land. I travelled up with an interesting young woman called Angela from Coombe who later joined the Sufis.

I joined up with Sjafrudin Ahmed and Asikin Alwi who were in Bapak's party, which also consisted of Bapak's wife Ibu Sumari, her eldest daughter Rochanawati, Dr Zakir a psychiatrist who was the official translator for Bapak's talks, and his wife. It is possible that Rahayu and Ismana were also there. I was made to feel totally at home even though I was a bit shy.

I was invited to eat with them. This was to be my first experience of Indonesian soup. I witnessed Rochanawati tasting the soup which had been made for Bapak and then pouring it down the sink. Bapak had often talked about the state a woman should be in when cooking and how effectively this could restore the energy of her husband and family. Even so, this act somewhat shocked me with the *waste not want not* Scottish moral code instilled in me. It was not until I was very tired and hungry, after an 8-hour return journey to Newcastle, that I experienced what Bapak meant. Ibu Sumari had left some soup for us all and after a few spoonfuls I was wide awake and full of energy.

From our house in Edinburgh Bapak made various trips to other cities.

I remember the trip to Glasgow, standing in a room of about twenty rather stiff businessmen. I felt inhibited and stiff myself, not wanting to embarrass anyone with the sounds or movements of my latihan. Quite suddenly the thought entered my head "It is the latihan, it has nothing to do with ME, just let it go!" With that I was off. So free did I feel when I heard, or thought I heard, Bapak say "Stop", I went up to him and without any inhibition said "Did you say stop?" He said "No, go on". Afterwards I felt fresh, relaxed and able to be and feel myself. In fact, to be my <u>real</u> self and not the imaginary me.

So Subud came to Scotland and I was glad.

Christmas 1963

There is a stately four story building in the Queen Anne style which lies between the Palace of Hampton Court and the village of Hampton. At that time one side looked over Hampton Park with its green swards and many sycamore, beech and chestnut trees. On the other, was a lovely rose garden which stretched down to the ever-flowing river Thames. It had been owned by a certain Lord Bearsted, then commandeered by the army in the Second World War and eventually became a 35 bed obstetric hospital. It was then known as Bearsted House.

It became my home for six months as I endeavoured to learn the art and science of good GP obstetrics. I had only one night at home a week. I was perpetually tired as I could be called for a birth at any time of day or night.

My registrar and my guide for advice was in Kingston Hospital, five miles away and sometimes separated at night by the Thames valley fogs. My consultant was a useless Irishman taken up with his private practice, whose standard piece of advice was to "Give her a touch of morphia boy!" But it was a wonderful privilege to witness so many births and to hear the cries of so many newborn babies.

We apparently appear from nowhere and at the end of our lives we disappear into nowhere. Or do we?

One evening in mid-December I went out into the garden to take a breather. I was very tired. I looked down across the rose garden to the Christmas lights strung along the banks of the Thames and began contemplating the meaning of Christmas. I thought of the cynical use that business made of it, with carols sung over and over again until they became meaningless. I suddenly asked myself, "I wonder what Christ was really like?

My walking was brought to a stop and a sensation, a kind of vibration, began in the pit of my stomach. It went on and on until all tension, all worry and anxiety had gone. This sensation then rose through my chest and then on through my throat doing the same as it had done in my solar plexus. It eventually reached my brain whose activity was brought to a complete standstill. Shortly after, a sensation of total bliss, like golden rain, descended on me.

My views on Christmas have never been the same since. Beneath the stress and rush of Christmas shopping, through the cacophony of carols sung over again, outside the requirements of religious observance and beneath all the sometimes forced present-giving, there is a certain something. It is called the Christmas Spirit. Is this a recognition within us that there is indeed a Higher Power who wants us to be happy and that to be so, we need actively to love both each other and ourselves?

For me this experience indicated that Jesus Christ is still present in the world.

The Visit to Paris in 1964

In 1964 Britain was at war with Indonesia, which had attacked its ally Malaysia. So Bapak Muhammad Subuh could not come to the UK. Instead he went to Paris, and as many British Subud members as could make it, travelled there for a long weekend.

Our old friends, Eileen and Tony Bright-Paul, looked after our two young children Martin and Lorna. We gave Maryam Kibble and Dorothy Stein a lift to Paris in our Renault 4L. Hotel rooms had been booked and Lavinia, Rohana's mother, was booked into the room next to ours.

The flat that had been arranged for Bapak was not very large but somehow we all managed to fit in with him. Bapak gave talks and held latihan daily in a large hall.

This was an important time for ex-Gurdjieff students of John Bennett, because he was in the process of leaving Subud and returning to his old discipline of 'the Work', as he understood it. He was working on a theory of Systematics and I think he visited Paris at that time. In relation to that dilemma, Bapak did an unforgettable mime.

He took out a packet of cigarettes and put them on the table in front of him.

"Say this packet of cigarettes is God". He then put the packet in the upper pocket of his shirt just above his heart. Next he mimed John

Bennett looking everywhere for God. "But here all the time!" as he pats the packet of cigarettes in the upper pocket of his shirt.

As always, the feeling of happiness that came from being with Bapak and his family was just so strong.

The next event is one I will never forget. Varindra was sitting next to Bapak and I was sitting directly opposite. I wanted to ask Bapak about the meaning of the Pentecost in relation to the coming of Subud but Varindra asked a question before I could. It was about the meaning of the story of Adam's rib. I hardly listened so intent was I to get my question in. At the end of Bapak's talk he looked directly across at me and said,

"You will never achieve your aim in life if you think too much."

I was furious. Why was he saying this to me in front of all these people when I already knew this was a personal weakness? I drove around Paris at about 100 mph, endangering everyone, I was so enraged.

I woke up the next morning and began thinking about it and then said to myself "Stop it!" And it did.

From then on my behaviour improved, at least for that glorious weekend. Our third child was conceived, the most self-disciplined and best behaved of all six of them.

The other seed planted that weekend was the wish and intention to go to Indonesia and spend time near to Bapak.

Yellow Taxi

I had visited Bapak's home in Cilandak in December 1966 shortly after obtaining my higher degree in medicine that would allow me various choices in life. I had gone there to get quiet and "receive" as best as I could the next stage of the family's life and mine. When I saw my old friend Sjafrudin I was surprised he suggested I should ask Bapak since he was also one who was in favour of receiving for one's own self.

Bapak said, "Go to New Zealand."

Shortly after returning to the UK I had one of those deep clear dreams that I can never forget and which on looking back gave me the energy and the determination to do things that I would not ordinarily do.

In the dream I saw Bapak standing beside a yellow taxi at the back of his house in Wisma Subud. He was putting his mother into the taxi and he needed some help. There were a few people around him whom I recognised as Subud brothers and sisters who were then living at Wisma Subud. I was standing behind and outside this circle of people around him, when Bapak looked at me and beckoned me with his finger to come and help him. I obeyed and as I helped him carry his mother into the taxi, my Inner feeling was immediately filled with a sense of the sacred, a mixture of sorrow and joy - the sorrow of parting and the joy of something else.

When I woke I thought "This is about leaving my mother and my mother country."

The meaning of this dream became crystal clear only six to seven years later when I became Bapak's doctor. He asked me to look after his mother. She was a tall dignified Javanese woman who had lived independently in her house in Semarang for many years, doing her own shopping, and being mother and grandmother to her large family. She made occasional visits to the 'Big House' in Wisma Subud, before eventually coming to live permanently where I saw her for a number of problems. One interesting time was over her painful arthritic knees.

I suggested that perhaps she perform her five daily prayers sitting, rather than doing the full prostrations. Bapak agreed but she was not going to be bossed by her son and simply said that life was not worth living if she could not do her prayers fully and properly.

When she was about ninety-seven years of age she became ill. I don't think she had ever been to a doctor before me and she was not really used to the idea of seeing doctors and was not willing to have tests or investigations, even simple physical examination was distasteful to her. Bapak wanted her to live and fully expected her to live until a hundred! Muti his granddaughter, then aged about seventeen, said, "Bapak has really got to let go of his mother," a statement at that time I judged to be somewhat cheeky and out of place.

Her true name is Ibu Kursinah. At this point I just seem to remember her as Eyang, Javanese for Granny. She refused food and eventually liquids and when I put drips up she pulled them out. It was clear that she wanted to go. "Life was no longer worth living."

So one evening near to the magrib (evening) prayer the family gathered at her bedside. I was at the bottom of the bed looking directly at her. I remember Bapak, Haryono, Ismana, Sharif, Tuti, Muti and Rohana being there.

I watched her propped up on pillows and as she drew her last breath in, it was as if she handed herself over to the Almighty with complete trust and serenity, passing from this world into the next through a door that was within herself. If ever I had had doubts about the existence of the next World, I had none from then on. At that moment also, I remembered the dream of seven years previously. The year she died was also the year the yellow taxis started in Jakarta.

Looking back, I see a very clear connection between the dream and the direction that my life took. Life and Death were and are the issue, and the way I am in life will be very much as Death comes. If I cannot really 'let go' now, I won't then! So when someone gives an example of true 'letting go' it is an inspiration, lesson and help in my own life.

Bapak's mother Ibu Kursinah

Bapak's Doctor
in Indonesia

Why and How We Went to Indonesia in 1967

In 1957 I had been living at Coombe Springs for the previous three years as a medical student, going up and down to London to the medical school at Guys hospital. I was part of a community that was practicing Gurdjieff's ideas on self-development. We were about 30 people living in a large Edwardian house with about 7 acres of garden and woodland. It had a spring house down in the corner which originally had been built by Cardinal Wolsey in the 16th century to supply water to his palace at Hampton Court. We were all somewhat serious people, leading an intense type of life, with the aim of waking up and becoming more conscious of our actions and our behaviour. Our intensity meant we were lacking in humour and therefore in self-awareness which, ironically, was what we were striving for.

Our teacher John Bennett had been aware of this and had been searching around for a new direction for all of us. When he heard of Pak Subuh (Bapak) he invited him to come and stay at Coombe Springs and those who wished to, could join Subud.

The diagnosis of man's condition by Bapak was similar to Gurdjieff's ideas that man in his normal state is unaware of the forces which influence him. He is therefore unaware of the higher forces which could lead him to a life that is more happy, vital and aware. However, the response to this diagnosis lead to two entirely different spiritual paths. The Gurdjieff method is to use intense efforts, with a clear aim in mind. The Subud way is to surrender and trust in the power of God, and thereby access that sacred part of one's Self which can receive guidance. This allowing, surrendered state works a transformation within the Self that is not possible by the use of one's will. This process of surrender to the Great Life Force (which Bapak received to convey to those who seek such contact) is called 'latihan'.

Before the coming of Subud I had an intense inner experience which was to guide me through all the changes that were about to happen. I will not describe this now, as it is covered elsewhere[5] but the main change that happened to me was that I began to feel much happier and lighter in myself and more normal. I began to pay more attention to my medical studies and focus on becoming a practical and capable doctor.

At this time, I met an Indonesian of my own age called Sjafrudin Ahmed. He was accompanying Bapak as a Subud Helper. He was very natural, unassuming and uncomplicated, yet possessed of an inner calm and warmth. This was the first time in my life that I felt I had a brother, such was the openness and naturalness of his character. Although I had had friends in the past, I had never felt such a deep connection with someone. A number of us felt drawn to him and visited him often in his little flat in the west wing of the house.

My life's journey had suddenly taken another direction. From being rather bleak, pessimistic and severe, life was now full of hope and a certain kind of beauty, warmth and affection. It was from this feeling that the wish to go to Indonesia arose. It seemed to me then Indonesia was the source of this new experience. It took me a time to realise the latihan was possible to follow fully anywhere and was independent of a nationality, culture, religion or anything else.

---

[5] See 'Muhammad Subuh Dawn and Herald of a New Age'

Bapak lived at Coombe Springs for one year until the middle of 1958. It was a time when many of us felt light, happy and very connected with one another, as if some wonderful spirit had come upon us. I, at times, felt as if I was in love, but there was no woman that I was in love with. It is difficult to describe the sense of excitement and of both inner and outer happiness so many of us felt at that time. Life went on and Bapak went to visit many other countries in Europe. He then visited North and South America and finally other countries on his way back to Indonesia. I think this was the second time the aim of going to Indonesia entered into me. But first there was the practical matter of getting my degree in medicine, and later training as a doctor in hospital posts of different specialities. During my first registration year as a doctor, I started to go out with Rohana and the next year we married. We started a family and I worked in various training posts around London. I needed to get practical experience to become an independent general practitioner.

In 1964 Bapak came to Paris. At that time Indonesia was at war with Malaysia and because Britain was an ally of Malaysia, no one from Indonesia could go to Britain. The only way for British people to see Bapak was to go to Paris. We went by car across the channel and friends took care of our children Martin and Lorna. In Paris we met Bapak in his flat which we crowded into to share in listening to his talk. I think it was then the idea of going to Indonesia again arose in Rohana and I, but because of the war we were unable to go.

In 1966 we had a holiday in Bridport and there I had my 32nd birthday. Three couples, the Lasalles, the Popes and the Horthys, who we felt close to and who were also in Subud, came to celebrate my birthday with us. The Popes had already gone to live in Jakarta with Bapak, but because of the war had been advised to leave temporarily. They had gone to New Zealand for a while and then came on to England. They intended to return when it was possible.

Sharif Horthy also was keen to go and his wife Hartati had already been on a short visit.

Towards the end of that year I had passed my higher medical exams that allowed me to specialise. We asked ourselves where we wanted to be next, whether for me to specialise or to go into general practice, and whether it should be in Britain or somewhere abroad such as Australia or New Zealand. But I was also looking for a job nearer Indonesia where it would be easier to visit Bapak.

Earlier that year we had done a locum in a general practice in the Cotswolds. It was a beautiful area. The practice was very satisfying work with a local cottage hospital in which to admit and care for patients. A third of the day was visiting patients in their homes either in the countryside or in the local country town. In some ways it was idyllic but we both asked ourselves whether we would want to spend the rest of our lives in such a place? Rohana and I felt we would go to sleep, in terms of our development as human beings. We felt a need for adventure and that adventure lay towards the East.

Our small flat in Twickenham was now too small for us so we sold it and rented a large furnished house on Kingston Hill while looking for a house to buy. Several came up but each time, for some reason or other, it fell through. This added another dimension to the question of what next? At the end of 1966 we decided I should go out to Indonesia to find the space in myself to answer that question.

When I arrived I was met by Sjafrudin who asked me "Why has it taken you so long to come?" I told him my reason for coming, expecting that we might sit quietly together as we had five years before, and come up with some kind of answer. However, one evening when we were sitting together on Pak Usman's porch he asked Bapak what I should do and where I should go. In fact, I was a little miffed, since I had wanted to find out for myself.

However, Bapak's answer that we should go to New Zealand more than satisfied me. I had already some friends there and the medical system was financed partly by the state, partly insurance, and partly by payment from the patient. It felt to me to be a good system of medical care with incentives for the patient, the doctor and the state to work together for the improvement of health. I left Indonesia with a sense of direction, self-confidence and the energy that went with it.

When I returned home to the UK I had one of those clear dreams that one never forgets[6]. Its meaning did not become clear to me for another seven years, however it was prescient of what was to come and added to the general feel of getting myself and my family moving. At this point I should add that although Rohana and I had differing points of view on almost everything, in this we were entirely together. It was she who had nudged me on to complete my medical qualifications and it was she who agreed that I go to Indonesia on my own, even with three children and one on the way.

When I returned and continued my job as registrar in rheumatology at Fulham Hospital, I started to phone all the oil companies in London who were pumping oil in the Middle East. At last I found the Kuwait Oil Company which was looking for a medical specialist to relieve their Medical Director in Kuwait, who was due a holiday of three months. They thought I was a little young for this post but they split the administrative and clinical sides and gave me the clinical post of Internist. I asked them, instead of a return fare to the UK, would they agree to fly us all on to New Zealand, with a 6-week stopover in Jakarta. They agreed.

We landed in Jakarta in November 1967. We both had splitting headaches from the journey but a place had already been prepared for us by Mariam Kibble who was in charge of the guest house. Our

---

[6] See 'The Yellow Taxi'.

small flat consisted of two rooms, a shared bathroom and a veranda that was to be our sitting room/kitchen and dining room - no more than about 40 metres square in all. No hot water, or refrigerators or gas stoves, and of course no air-conditioners. But we were incredibly happy. I knew then I wanted to live there for a while.

It seemed there was a great opportunity to both grow as a human being and to become a doctor in the real sense of the word. That is, one who could use his knowledge to serve others, particularly those who did not have the means to access medical care.

This in fact was to happen, as the following stories reveal.

Subud helpers Asikis Alwi, Sjafrudin Ahmed,
Rachman Mitchell and Abdullah Pope

Pak Selamet's Picture of Us

I am lying back in the Swan River, five kilometre up from the sea in Fremantle, making the first few strokes of my morning swim. I'm looking at the leaves of trees lining the shore. They reflect the golden light of the dawn, and the branches that bear them are tilted slightly to the magnificent blue heaven above.

It evokes a memory of a painting done for us forty-nine years ago by Pak Selamet. He did several paintings for those of us who were on a particular inner and outer journey together in the Java of the late 1960s. His paintings were symbolic of each of our situations in life at that time. We were there to be opened to a new way of experiencing life, of finding and developing our talent to live in the world and yet remaining true to something beyond this world. The 'opener' was Bapak.

There is a Muslim prayer that starts with: *I surrender myself to the Lord of the Dawn.* When I awake early before sunrise, I sense the inspiration behind this prayer. Every day is a new day with different possibilities of change. We can change and grow. We don't have to go on repeating the same mistakes over and over again. It is possible to correct ourselves.

Everyone loved and respected Bapak. People came from all over the world to be inspired by him. He was careful to say he was not a guru, or a prophet. Simply Bapak, or Father, who shared his experience of being opened to the Great Life Force and purified by it. This allowed him to fulfil his mission in life, to share this experience with others who, in their turn, could share it with others too.

I think I met Pak Selamet the painter, an old friend of Bapak's, at the end of 1966. I had travelled to Indonesia on my own to find out whether we as a family should stay in England and work in a country practice, or go abroad. I asked him to do a painting for me. A year later I saw the painting. It was of me in Javanese dress, holding the bridle of a horse by a beach. In front was moored a small wooden rowing boat. Behind were these lovely trees with the dawn light on them. The sun on the horizon was to the left and on the right was a beautiful white sailing ship.

The symbolism was clear. I was about to sail off somewhere and at that moment it seemed we were going to New Zealand.

I showed this painting to my wife Rohana who asked, "Why am I not in it?"

So I took it back to Pak Selamet explaining I had a wife and family. He later presented me with a new painting. The horse had a beautiful woman on it, and I was leading it. She was holding a large pot (the symbol that she was pregnant with our younger son Sachlan). The ship had gone, although the small boat was still there. Over the water there was a magnificent mountain with a temple on it.

I felt safe in leaving Rohana and the children in the safety of Wisma Subud while I went to New Zealand doing locums. I was fasting twice a week to help me find a job in Java. That way I could stay close to the man who inspired us. I was successful. I became doctor for the British Embassy, and later for half the expatriate community of Jakarta.

So the sailing ship did turn into the temple on the mountain, and this beautiful picture was an accurate foretelling of the course of my life for the next 15 years.

Ah… it's good to have a morning swim and to be in the Now which contains the past, the present, and the future.

The Meaning and Purpose of Fasting

Shortly after arriving in Wisma Subud, in December 1967, I experienced my first Ramadan. Each night we men would gather together in the entrance space to the latihan hall to become quiet in ourselves. After latihan we would sit with Bapak. Often when we became quiet enough, he would begin to talk, always in Indonesian, sometimes there was translation into English and sometimes not. In a way it did not matter, because the feelings were being moved to receive something for ourselves. There was, however, something direct for me one night.

Bapak asked me to stand up with Asikin Alwi to test the meaning and purpose of following the Ramadan fast. I received it was to deepen my worship of Almighty God, and Bapak added it was also to intensify the purification of one's self, a kind of 'spring clean'.

It was common for people at that time to fast on Mondays and Thursdays. In Indonesian, this was called 'prihatin', and it is a form of self-restraint or self discipline. Bapak asked me to stand and receive what was the purpose of that kind of fasting. I received fairly clearly it was to make me strong but he added it was also to achieve an aim one had set oneself, such as to gain a particular job or to get further up in one's career path.

I decided at that point to fast Mondays and Thursdays for the next six months in order to get a job, which would enable me to live in Wisma Subud. In this I was ultimately successful. [7]

---

[7] See 'Pak Selamat's Picture of Us'.

Bapak Smiled

It was May 1968 and Bapak was visiting Auckland for the New Zealand Congress. I was working as a GP while Rohana and the children were living in Wisma Subud in Indonesia.

I went to the airport to meet the party and help transport the baggage to the ferry which would take them to the home of Erling Week, on Waiheke Island in the Haurake Gulf.

Sungkum is an old Javanese custom of paying respect to someone such as your parents whom you love. We expatriate Subud members had spontaneously adopted this Javanese custom as a sign of our respect and love for Bapak. It was only a month or two back that I had knelt to sungkum Bapak before I had left Wisma Subud. Thus, as Bapak walked through the glass doors of the airport, I went down on my knees, took his hand and kissed it. Immediately there was a whack across my shoulders from Bapak's rolled up newspaper as if to say, "That is not appropriate here".

I piled the entire luggage into my Renault 4L and made my way to the ferry café on Queen Street. Here Bapak was sitting in one of those enclosed seated tables with Pak Usman and Erling Week opposite him. There was a spare seat beside Bapak where he indicated I should sit. He passed me a custard pie and began to talk about my parents-in-law coming to New Zealand. His body language message seemed to be saying "Relax and be normal in conformity with your surroundings, which is now New Zealand".

Waiheke was and is of course a beautiful Island but for me it will never be as beautiful and alive as it was then in May 1968. At the time I write this, the house of Erling Week (later Mark) is still there, perched overlooking the incoming jetty for the ferry.

Our meetings, latihan and talks by Bapak were held in the village hall down in the valley. At the end of one latihan I sat in one of the chairs scattered about. I was transported by the latihan, which seemed to me to go deeper and wider than ever and filled me with the utmost bliss. I looked up and saw Bapak smiling at me, as if to say how incredibly fortunate we are to have received this Gift.

Jaga Malam and the Golden Umbrella

1967 to 1969 were wonderful years of my life. I had hardly any possessions, money or material security, yet happiness in spades and a feeling of development both inner and outer.

The physical centre of it lay in a building, the old latihan hall of Wisma Subud. That one-story building lay at right angles to the main potholed road of Jalan Rumah Sakit Fatmawati. It was about 50 metres from the road and separated by Bapak's newly built house and garden. Its roof was of terra cotta tiles, the walls of white washed breeze-blocks and the floors of grey tiles.

The first part, just under a quarter of it, was an entrance hall with the secretariat offices to one side. In one corner of the entrance hall was a very simple armchair, with a table both in front and at the side. This was Bapak's chair where he would sit most evenings.

Through a double door entrance one reached the latihan hall, large enough for about 50 people to do latihan freely. The building then went on further to house the family of Pak Sudarto on the right, and Pak Prio Hartono on the left, members of Bapak's secretariat.

The years 1964 to 1966 had been a period of great political and social turbulence for Indonesia, with the end of Bung Sukarno's presidency. In particular, there had been a struggle between the

74

army and the communist party and an estimated one million had lost their lives. The Subud compound, with its known relations to Westerners, was on the elimination list of the communist party. One wealthy American brother (Erling Week later Mark) had been held up at night and robbed.

Hence the practice of a night watch or jaga malam had developed. In one sense it was a purely practical action to prevent intruders. It also had another meaning, an inner one. The Javanese custom of staying up at night, and doing without sleep, was a kind of self-discipline prihatin or prayer to ward off danger.

Although by the time I arrived in November 1967 the danger seemed mostly over, the custom of jaga malam continued as 20 to 30 of us gathered in the entrance hall of the latihan building each night. What could have been a duty and responsibility was a pleasure. What pleasure? The pleasure of Bapak's company. Again an inner and outer experience. He would tell stories, make jokes sometimes test with us, but what we really came for was the inner boost to our own latihan, which raised us temporarily to a deeper and higher level within ourselves. I remember now the sound of the cicadas, their collective vibrations going louder then softer, seeming to match what was happening in our own feelings. It was as if the cicadas knew how we were and were in tune with us. Often we went to bed at 3 am and woke at 6 am, feeling quite fresh.

My family lived in skid row, named because it was fairly basic, but also because banana skins were occasionally thrown onto the concrete path outside. Our four (later five) children were in two bunk beds in one room. There was no gas or electric stoves, fridges or air-conditioners. Getting cool was done by throwing water over one's body, 3 or 4 times a day. Everyone was thin. I went from 90 to 67 kg in a short time. Butter, milk and meat were still luxuries. The years blot out the difficulties of adjusting to a new culture and climate, all that comes back is the feeling of closeness between us all, irrespective of class, nationality, wealth or education. We called ourselves the Subud Brotherhood, a term which included men, women and children.

One night while staying up with Bapak, I was called out to attend a patient who had fallen and injured his shoulder while attempting to climb a flagpole in a drunken state. It was indeed like going from heaven into a kind of hell.

In Javanese culture there is the symbol of the Golden Umbrella, which represents the Grace or Wahyu, which has fallen on a certain person. I think many of us were drawn to gather and shelter under this umbrella of Bapak's.

There were many tests that Bapak did with us to try and make us aware of certain spiritual realities. For me these tests seemed to indicate I was still in kindergarten spiritually.

This account of those days may not convey enough the strange contrast of the intimacy with Bapak yet at the same time the feeling he was far above us, in purity, awareness and understanding.

When, after a year, I was able to open my clinic, he came and inspected it, weighed himself on the scales and congratulated me. He suggested a selamatan for the future of the clinic and he chose a part of the Wayang to be danced by the Sudarsono family. This took place in the latihan hall, where Bapak prayed that Indonesia would become our home.

In 1969 Bapak's talks became more and more centred on Enterprise and bringing the spiritual into the material. The days of gathering under the Golden Umbrella with him were over. It was up to each one of us to follow our own latihan with sincerity, patience, trust and courage and to find the best way to put it into practice in our lives.

You Can Play the Violin
and the Piano Too

We had arrived in Jakarta in November 1967 to stay in the Wisma Subud compound, which was Bapak's home. We were his guests, or rather one of his extended family. We all had this embracing feeling of being part of his family.

As I have already explained there was much unrest in the country due to the political situation. As a result, there was a custom at night of 'jaga malam', that is to stay up and keep guard. Bapak was part of this and would receive and talk about the spiritual life. Since this was Indonesia, and specifically Java, it was in reference often to the ancient Javanese culture.

It is difficult to convey the atmosphere because these were not just interesting talks. We were conveyed to a deeper and a lighter part of ourselves and at the same time became closer to one another and to Bapak. We began to sense Bapak's love for us and to reciprocate. But there was no doubt about who was the Father and who were the Children.

These evenings had almost stopped by 1970. After the death of Ibu Sumari in early 1971 they only took place on two Fridays of the month for the Helpers. Sometime later that year, Bapak held a meeting at Wisma Indonesia in an open Pendopo area, where the local South Jakarta group ordinarily had its meetings and office. He asked us whether there was anything we would like to ask before he went on another world journey to visit the Subud groups in various countries. I have noted in myself there is often a gap, sometimes a very large gap, between my ordinary understanding and my inner understanding based on what I really know from my own experience. What was about to happen revealed that. It also revealed something else in apparent contradiction.

I said, "Would Bapak like the Helper's group to meet while he was away and test member's questions"?

'Yes," said Bapak "and you can take the meetings and play the violin and the piano too!!!"

Bapak could be very sharp in order to show something. I am a slow learner and the words have echoed in my mind over many years, until I really saw the ridiculousness, the impossibility of recreating anything like we experienced in the Helpers meetings with him.

There was shocked silence when dear Ismana said, "But Bapak the women meet when you are away." No answer.

Then Professor Hazirin a Sumatran and a Professor of Islamic Law said, "What is going to happen to Subud when you die?" - a question few others would have dared to ask.

Bapak then asked Ismana to get up and test or receive an answer to that question.

She stood up and her body was moved to spin gently and her arms slowly came up and her fingers vibrated gently. The feeling that seemed to envelop all of us was the essential 'grace' that enveloped Bapak inwardly and outwardly, was and would continue to be, in all of us, and in fact, in everything.

Although, this was a 'put down' to my cockiness, and lack of respect that what Bapak had been receiving with us on these Friday nights, was indeed of a high and miraculous order, it at the same time created the opportunity for testing which revealed each of us was connected to 'something' in him that was eternal.

Likewise, I see now for me personally this correction of my ignorance and arrogance was also a kindness.

Dr Jaka

I first met Dr Jaka in 1968 in his office as Secretary General of Health for the Indonesian Government, after my return from New Zealand in June.

Rohana, I and our 4 children had arrived in Indonesia about a year earlier to be with Bapak. All of us, despite the poor external conditions, felt very much at home and alive. I was excited to be in on the early development, as I thought, of both the material and social life of Indonesia.

On my return from New Zealand Rohana told me the British Ambassador wanted to see me to ask if I would set up a clinic for British businessmen returning to Indonesia after the Konfrontasi war between Malaysia and Indonesia. This conflict had been wasteful on the country's resources, and the new Suharto government were keen to attract foreign western investment back again to help build up the country after a long period of misrule. I was then asked to meet with the British businessmen's group who also asked me to set up a medical practice to serve them and their families. In order to do this, I needed to get the permission of the Department of Health. Hence my meeting with Dr Jaka.

He explained that since the Dutch withdrew all their doctors from Indonesia, it had been a policy to forbid foreign doctors to practice in Indonesia.

It is interesting how and why an apparent brick wall in front of one suddenly collapses. I sat there quietly for a moment, at the same time feeling very alive. "I love this country," I said, "and I want to contribute in any way that I can to its development".

Dr Jaka suddenly became rather quiet himself for a minute.
"There is a way that you can stay and work here," he said. "You can set up your clinic in any Embassy. Embassy ground is not under Indonesian rules, but you must not see Indonesian patients".

The way would develop later for me to be of some help to the poorer section of the local community but for now this was a means for me to look after my family, continue to live in the Wisma Subud compound, and to be of service to my friends living there. I felt profoundly grateful to this man who for some reason was touched by my appeal to him and reacted in a human way. As long as Dr Jaka was Secretary General, I was safe and secure.

Some years later I met him again. He was attending a selamatan for the opening of a Rehabilitation Centre next to the Fatmawati Hospital in Cilandak and, as is the custom, he was sitting on the ground. He indicated for me to sit beside him. I think he knew of my interest in rehabilitation. That was one of my specialities before I became a GP, I used to meet doctors who came from abroad under the Care program, to teach young Indonesian orthopaedic surgeons.

He told me that he had been feeling rather flat and asked himself why? The answer that came to him was that he had not given enough to the community and as he happened to have a piece of land near to the hospital he had decided to donate it as part of his 'amal'[8] for the community.

It was on this land that the new Rehabilitation Centre had been built and the reason for the selamatan taking place.

---

[8] Amal means putting into practice religious and communal responsibilities to be mindful of the needs of others and, while acting in a humble way, to meet those needs if possible.

A Home at Last

When I returned from New Zealand to Jakarta, in June 1968, my family had moved into a new lodgings opposite our old one. This consisted of three rooms and a long veranda with a bathroom at the end of it. The veranda looked out onto the gardens of the house next door where there were chickens and a monkey. We were separated from them by a one and a half metre high brick wall with an iron trellis above it. Living continued to be simple as I've described before but we did purchase a kerosene fridge, which was a great improvement.

At the beginning of 1969 my practice had begun and occasionally the patients would call by for medical purposes. Sometimes they would catch me with a towel around my waist going to the bathroom at the end of the veranda to have a 'mandi' or shower. It seemed a little inappropriate as they, at this time, were already living quite well, with air-conditioned home and chauffeur driven cars.

So one day when Bapak passed our lodgings I asked him when I could start to build our house. He asked, what the hurry was, and I described how my patients would sometimes find me with a towel around my waist. He immediately understood and we walked together down the path to the bottom of the compound. When we reached the bottom fence Bapak put his heel in the ground next to a large cashew nut tree and said, "Rachman should have 1000 square metres or so to build his house here".

The land was paid for with money I had earned in New Zealand (USD$500). The money to build the house was paid for by the Medical Scheme, which had already raised money from companies that registered their employees with me. The cost was ten thousand pounds sterling, which seems a very small amount now but it built a very nice house of about 275 square metres.

I was impatient for the building to be finished, but there were always long delays. Pak Usman was the one who was in charge of our building. He was also Bapak's Treasurer and money came in and money went out of one pot. It was difficult for me to understand and be patient, as at that time, I had limited understanding of how a tight budget affected the flow of money and a strong western material point of view of 'what is mine is mine'!

Eventually after seeing how discontented I was, Bapak's eldest son took over and our house was finished at the end of 1969. Ours was in fact the first house to be built in the new part of the compound. The selamatan for our house warming was in January 1970 arranged by Bapak's wife Ibu Sumari.

The Mitchell family in Wisma Subud- Sachlan, Lorna, Rohana, Isabella, Lydia, Rachman, Maria. Eldest son Martin is away.

The Road to Suka Mulia

It is forty-nine years since I first visited this place, high up in the hills of Sunda in West Java. We were in an old jeep, and I was sitting with my back up against its sides. With me were a New Zealander and an Indonesian, both close friends from Subud.

The roads were potholed and narrow, as we drove from Jakarta through Bogor, and on the through the mountainous countryside that led up through the tea plantations to Puncak. We continued over the pass and down, winding by, holiday homes where families came to rest over the weekend, like Girinadi. This once belonged to the British Embassy and we stayed there in our early days, for a weekend or two. Then down past a road where Lambert Gibbs, Robin Jones, the Lentkes and the Roberts once had cottages. Down to the bridge over a rocky ravine, where a bus out of control had once plunged over into the river below. Up again and turn to the left. The images and memories all come back again of those fifteen years in which we visited and savoured that place on holidays and weekends with our children.

My first evening there forty-nine years ago, I can still remember with clarity. In those times the holiday places were only a few, and very old, from the Dutch times. Everyone was poor. Even then, I delighted in the countryside that was spread out before us, paddy fields, fields of vegetables and always the sound of running water. Sundanese music often begins with the sound of running water, then the sound of birds singing, then a steady rhythm, a beat before the human voice comes in to sing in harmony, rejoicing in the sounds of nature and the feeling of connection. Suling is the name of the melody. It is lovely.

On that first trip, it was another 25 minutes into the countryside, driving on rougher and rougher roads before we finally reached Suka Mulia at sunset. The group of pines marked the entrance as they still do today. As we went through, we could see a long bamboo house with woven bamboo walls and a red tile roof on our left. This was where the selamatan, for the success of the farm, was to be held that evening. It would be followed by a wayang golek, (a wooden puppet show from Wayang stories) for the entertainment of the local villagers and us foreigners.

Prayers were first said by the local imam and next food baskets passed around for us all to share. Then the Wayang began. This was the first time I had ever heard the music or the stories. They are an integral part of both Javanese and Sundanese culture. The latter music seems to flow with a greater energy, reflecting perhaps the cooler air and the constant sound of running water - like my own Highlands of Scotland. The stories come from the Mahabharata but have been modified by muslim saints in the past.

There was no electricity then in the countryside and no gas. Lighting was by kerosene lamps and the gentle hiss that they gave off would mix with the sound of the dalang puppeteer. He sang the story of the Pendawas (the goodies) against the Kurawas (the baddies), the perennial struggle of human life.

There was a box on either side of the Dalang. On his right was the box for the Pendawa puppets, on his left was the box for the Kurawas. Around 10 pm I noticed a little boy no older than three, fast asleep in the box with the Pendawas. It was all very new to me but I was enjoying the new pentatonic music and the story, which I could only partly understand from the gestures of the puppets. Everyone was relaxed and happy.

Bapak had bought the land with the help of money from overseas Subud members, particularly the Tokyo group who had been very generous. He had encouraged us to help in the development of Indonesia and he suggested that a dairy farm be started. Milk and butter were very short then. Almost everyone was thin. Even top government officials, but not Sukarno the President, of course.

I woke at about 8 am on a bamboo palette clean but firm, the pentatonic music still beating in my head, the smell of wood fire smoke in my nostrils. Gas bottles were not yet a feature of cooking in the mountains and kerosene was too expensive for most country people. There was another smell almost impossible to describe, the wet earthiness of Sundanese country life.

Ibu Sumari's half-brother Pak Handoyo was already living up in Cipanas, and shortly after we had started living in Cilandak, we used to go up to stay with him and his family. There again, the sounds and smells of Sunda country life would envelop us and refresh us.

Gifts From Bapak

It was not long after we had moved into our new house in Wisma Subud in 1970 there was a knock on the door on a Sunday morning between 7 and 8. It was followed by a call of 'Cooee' several times. Being Sunday, Rohana and I had decided to have a bit of a sleep in, but something caused me to get up and go downstairs.

It was Bapak come to pay us a visit and to suggest a few things to us.

His brother-in-law Pak Handoyo had found five hectares of land near the mountain town of Cipanas. We had already spent several weekends there as guests of him and his wife in their two-story house on the side of the dusty, pebbled road that led to fields of carrots and other vegetables further up the mountain side of Gunung Gede. We found the sounds of country life around, with the views of the mountains in the distance and the cool air, very refreshing.

Bapak suggested that we team up with four other families. His daughter Hardiyati, the Popes, the Winklers and the Horthy's so that we all could spend time together and benefit from the cooler climate.

"Grow cabbages, keep cows and horses' he said

I, at first, was not used to the thought of managing that amount of land and said a thousand square metres would be fine.

"No! You need a hectare. Spread yourselves out".

This was very different to the learning of doing without of the previous three years, where everyone was very poor and we were living on top of one another.

I think Pak Usman, Bapak's translator at that time, was with us and cups of tea were being sipped as I was slowly taking this all in. I am still very slow off the mark and did not realise all the happiness that would come to us as a family by our spending time together and also with our friends at our Cipanas home over the next twelve years.

But more was to come in terms of a certain gift of happiness. In this the memories of Rohana and mine differ as to which visit these words were spoken.

"How many children do you have?" Bapak asked us, but his eyes were on Rohana.

"Five, Bapak".

"You should have two more children" Bapak said.

"No Bapak I can't, I have had five children in the last eight years"

There was a pause. An inner silence hung there and then Bapak spoke quite differently as he did when receiving.

"When it is the Will of God that you should have more children, you should follow.

Shortly after Bapak got up and left.

A few months later I was sitting on the floor beside Bapak's chair at the Hal bil halal celebration at the end of Ramadan. Bapak said to me, "You should not be afraid of having more children Rachman". That night Isabella our youngest daughter was conceived. The spirit of joy and happiness was intense.

Nine months later her birth took place just as the 1971 Congress was ending when there were over 2000 people staying in the compound with 17 guests staying in our house sleeping on the floor or in spare bedrooms. The mood as in many Congresses was joyful, even euphoric. The notes of a beautiful piece of cello music played by Leslie Parker were floating out of our latihan hall on the last night of the Congress.

According to Rohana I gave her an injection of Pethidine saying that I needed a good night's sleep before a full day's work the next day. That was not the way I remember it, however, strong labour pains started soon after midnight and I called our friend and neighbour Lydia Duncan who had been a midwife in her early years who bundled herself into the car with Rohana. We drove through the night to St Carolus hospital where Rohana had been booked in. We got to the hospital just in time and Isabella was born on arrival.

The feeling of joy which we had experienced at her conception returned again.

Ibu Sumari

Of all the people I have met in my life Ibu Sumari is one I feel particularly grateful I knew.

She was one for whom the common title, Ibu or Mother, was truly apt. Over the time I knew her, I began to feel her maternal care for me and my family and I began to respond to that as any son would. Many others who came to Wisma Subud also experienced her motherliness.

If I say Ibu Sumari was/is a great soul, few who knew her would disagree. She had two children by her previous marriage, her daughter Rochanawati and a son who I knew nothing of until he turned up at her funeral in early 1971. It was rumoured he had been a communist and had needed to lie low.

Ibu Sumari had come to Bapak as a pupil seeking a spiritual teacher in mid-1941 when Bapak was a widower with four children. Their meeting and later marriage is very simply and beautifully related in his autobiography.

When we first arrived in Jakarta in November 1967 with four children and Rohana pregnant with our fifth child Sachlan, it was intended to be just a six-week stopover on our way to New Zealand. When Rohana asked Bapak whether she could have the baby in Jakarta, Bapak replied that he would answer later.

Soon he called Rohana and said she could stay in Wisma Subud with the children and I should go on to New Zealand to earn the money to look after my family staying in Cilandak.

Ibu Sumari took Rohana under her wing arranging for Ibu Susila to oversee her medical care. She also expected Rohana to call on her every morning to make sure all was well with her and the children.

When our house was finished at the end of 1969, it was Ibu Sumari who arranged the Selamatan. It was the custom to hold a 'selamatan' to pray for the well-being of the family that would live in the house and for good neighbourly feeling toward the local community around it. She arranged the food for the gathering in our house for everyone living in or visiting Wisma Subud to be eaten after prayers were said by the local Imam. It was a happy and memorable event. She had really helped us on the path to relating well with our new Indonesian neighbours.

Ibu said that I was 'berani'. That means both bold and courageous. I was aware that I could be bold, impatient and somewhat unmannered in the exquisitely sensitive world of Javanese manners. It is possible she might have felt it took courage to make a step into the 'unknown' country still insecure and poor. However, those thoughts did not occur to us, we were so grateful to be bathed in the atmosphere that surrounded Bapak and Ibu.

Ibu began to use me as her doctor. She had diabetes and at that time there was no self-monitoring of blood glucose. I felt I was already being over 'bold' when I suggested that she leave off the sweet drinks and sugar in her tea.

An event took place in 1970 that no one who attended will ever forget. It was a party given by Bapak to celebrate Ibu's birthday which none of us knew would be her last. He encouraged us all to relax, to let go and to sing our favourite songs. Several of us sang or played instruments. Then Bapak began to sing. It was a different kind of song altogether which touched our feelings in a deeper place. It seemed to bring us all closer together and closer to Bapak.

The party went on till four in the morning and we went home "as fresh as daisies", light and happy, and only needed a few hours sleep to begin the day. I can say unreservedly it was the best party I have ever been to. There is a photo of Bapak and Ibu sitting together, Bapak leaning towards her which is how I remember them at that party.

One day she got tonsillitis and despite antibiotics her state began to rapidly deteriorate. I noticed the increase in her glucose and presence of ketones in her urine which meant she could go into a diabetic coma at any moment. I wanted to send her into hospital where her biochemistry could be monitored. In Indonesia, in those days, hospitals for most people were places where people went to die. Bapak's answer to me was that Ibu would prefer to stay at home with him and that anyhow she would not die just yet. I really did not know enough about the main hospital to argue with Bapak and anyhow felt he must be right.

Sadly, this was not so. Within a short time Ibu slipped into a coma and I was called to the house just as her heart had stopped and immediately began to carry out CPR. Bapak came into the room at that moment and I seemed to see an expression of surprise on his face.

This whole episode is very well described by Lusanna Faliks.[9]

---

[9] This is available in video and CD format and can be sourced from various online bookshops.

I wondered then and for some years later whether I had been 'berani' enough to explain clearly and in detail to Bapak why I had recommended Ibu go into hospital. It is always like that when one's patient dies. Did I do enough? Could things have gone differently if I had done my job properly? In the end it felt impertinent to enquire any further, as I felt in my deeper Self it was her Destiny to die then. Alhumdullilah.

Ibu Sumari

A Roll of Thunder

While Bapak was alive, he frequently reminded us to read Susila Budhi Dharma. The original was a poem received by him in High Javanese and was accompanied by beautiful melodies in the classical Javanese style. However, the meaning still came through in the Bahasa Indonesia that Bapak himself translated it into. Of course, great care was taken to get the English translation right.

It seemed that Bapak wished us to have an understanding of the process of development that the latihan was carrying us through. "Don't be satisfied with just making movements and uttering sounds but go deeper and become aware of their origin and their purpose."

In a moment of apparent resignation later he said in the mid-80s, "If you forget everything I have told you, just continue your latihan and you will find the truth for yourself."

It is clear however that he did not give talks for fun, or just to be close to us. He explained over and over again the meaning, the benefit and the process of the latihan. He hoped that we Helpers would understand also and assist him in the spread of the latihan to ALL Mankind.

I was in the Wisma Subud latihan hall one Sunday when Bapak was giving a talk, when again he advised us all to read Susila Budhi Dharma. A question arose from a young Indonesian member.

"You have written about the four lower worlds of forces, why have you not written about the three worlds above those?"

At that moment there was the sound of something like a roll of thunder and we were all shaking. It was Bapak being angry and shouting,

"Stand up you there! If you are not aware of the working and the influence of these lower forces on you, you will never ascend or become aware of these higher worlds of forces!"

So why did Bapak give these talks and why did he advise us to read or listen to them? Indeed, **how** should we read and listen to them? Sometimes when I am reading or listening I say to myself, "I ought to already understand this for myself, but I don't." Then I feel so grateful for the guidance he is giving to my understanding - which wants to appear to know what it really doesn't know yet.

Walking and the Zikr

Occasionally Bapak would ask us whether we had any experiences "outside the normal" which gave us evidence or proof of the latihan kejiwaan (the training of our soul) in our selves. I think he wanted evidence for himself as well, that we were making progress.

One Ramadan he again asked this question. "Has anyone experienced something new in this Ramadan, some evidence from your fasting of God's gift to you?"

One person said he had seen the Four Horsemen of the Apocalypse. Bapak did not comment, just asked if there were any others. Why I decided to mention my experience I do not know, because in a way it was something seemingly not so significant.

I said "I was walking around the latihan hall at 1 am in the morning on the 21st night of Ramadan when suddenly I experienced a feeling of happiness in my legs, which made me feel very light."

"Get up and show me" Bapak said.

Difficult to re-experience that again, but I had a try to receive again.

"Yes," Bapak said "That is the zikr, that is your legs worshipping God. That is also the way for you to cure yourself when you are ill."

Where is Your Head?

There are tests I experienced with Bapak, which showed me something that was really valuable for my life.

I knew my habit of thinking, which was not really thinking, but a constant inane chatter in my head blocked my awareness and perception of what was going on. I was also skeptical about testing. One could say I was 'hard headed' despite having very free latihans that left me happy with a feeling of well-being.

Bapak was not above giving one of his many children a thump to wake them up. But I was obstinate. I was not going to give up on my skepticism until I had proof that testing was a tool for self-awareness, self-correction and self-development.

It requires being a child again with all the openness, awe and honesty that there is within us all.

So, in a Sunday talk in the Wisma Subud latihan hall, with about a hundred and fifty people seated, I am called to the front. Bapak is in his chair, as always, relaxed. Within reach is a glass of water with a glass of tea, put there by Muti his granddaughter. He is giving a talk on the development of the human mind.

"Come to the front Rachman"
"Relax""
"Where is your head?"

"Have you received?"

"No", I answer.

"Receive again. Where is your head?"

"Have you received?"

I thank the Almighty that Bapak had the patience with me to go on, because patience is what I needed at that moment. I also needed a sense that something can change in me, so I can grow as a person. Whatever was happening to make me let go, it did happen, maybe on the third or fourth attempt.

Suddenly, I sensed my own presence in my brain. At first it seemed mostly in the front of my brain. Then Bapak's testing of me seemed to go deeper, as he took anatomical slices through my brain, to the mid part and then to the back. I was on a journey in my own brain. It had become a friend instead of a bother. Finally, when this very pleasant state in my brain seemed complete, Bapak said,

"And now let your mind blend with the Universal mind"

I cannot remember that state at all. All I remember, as I type this account of some 40 years ago, is my whole body shaking and the tears flowing down my cheeks. My arrogance had been humbled and my idea of myself had been recast.

I could hear Bapak chuckling in the background saying "Yah, yah, Rachman could not even remember his family in that state."

Selamatan for John Godolphin Bennett

There had been a dividing of the paths after the initial huge expansion in the numbers of people being opened in Subud in the late 1950s and early 1960s. John Bennett saw very clearly that there was no place for him as a teacher in Subud. In his book 'Concerning Subud' he had prophesied that Subud would spread to millions of people. Perhaps he began to doubt that Subud would in fact benefit mankind.

He was looked up to by many in the Gurdjieff movement and as a result of his disillusionment with Subud, he had returned to the Gurdjieff Work and began to give lectures on the Work again. He handed in his Subud Helper's card. His letters to Bapak at this time make interesting reading and Bapak's reply is very touching.

So, some of his former pupils felt he had let the Subud side down. However, many of us felt we owed a great debt to him. Firstly, for being the means of bringing us to Subud and secondly for all his kindness and care in the years that we were his pupils living at Coombe Springs.

Certainly his influence on us had been great. He was a serious man given to contemplation of the state of mankind, set out very well in his books 'Crisis in Human Affairs' and 'What Are We Living For?'

He had vast knowledge both in the world of Science and Psychology and in the esoteric past.

But it seemed to me he was not happy. For a time after he was opened and Bapak came to stay at Coombe Springs, Bennett was deliriously happy. He laughed a lot. He was like a little boy. It was a huge change for us to witness this in a person who, we thought, was a man of exceptional spiritual attainment. In a sense what we were witnessing then was the difference between his Essence and his Personality as a spiritual teacher which he had explained himself so many times.

One day I attended my Gurdjieff group meeting at which Bennett said we must not forget the principles of the Work and the lessons of the past. To my astonishment I found myself saying "No! All has changed. Our Teacher is within us and it is to that, we must listen". It astonished Bennett as well.

I was already part of a small group that met around Sjafrudin Ahmed, the Indonesian Helper who Bapak had left behind at Coombe. Sjafrudin's role was to see that the practice of the latihan was kept according to Bapak's guidance. A dividing line between the Work and the practice of the latihan began to exist at Coombe. It was uncomfortable but necessary.

I jump now to the early 1970's. I was living in Wisma Subud when we heard of Bennett's death. I went to Bapak and asked whether we should have a selamatan to pray for the welfare of the soul of John Bennett? Bapak's answer was unforgettable:

"It is never wrong to pray for someone's soul. Whether the prayer is effective depends on the willingness of the person being prayed for to receive it and the sincerity of the person making the prayer. Therefore, Bapak will come to the selamantan and will also say something about John Bennett."

The selamatan took place in our house and was attended by Bennett's old pupils, and those who had known him, living in Wisma Subud. We were sitting in a circle and I had Sharif Horthy on my right and Bapak next to him. As the prayers got going I felt a deep sadness like a lump of lead gathering in the centre of my chest. When the prayers ended Bapak got up and left after about two minutes, whilst usually he would stay for half an hour or longer, and he did not say anything about John Bennett. Only Sharif seemed to feel as I did. Everyone else was happy with the selamatan.

Bapak has given very clear talks on the spiritual paths illustrated by Anwas and Anwar. In this story Anwas sought the Grace of God by his own intense efforts which included owning no material possessions, meditation and fasting. Anwar, however, simply received a Grace from the Almighty in measure with his faith and surrender. There was no conscious effort or desire. He received direct instruction from God and experienced an Ascension. I think John Bennett was probably well aware of the difference. It seems he could not help himself.

There is something else to add to this story which took place at the International Subud Congress at Anugraha in 1983. Bennett's widow, Elizabeth Bennett came. Bapak announced that before his death, John Bennett wrote to him asking for forgiveness and saying that he recognised the latihan was truly a Grace from Almighty God.

We have so far been unable to trace this letter. However, Rashid Carre said he was present when Bapak announced it one evening at a Helper's meeting in Wisma Subud and called for Sudarto to get the letter from the Secretariat. So presumably this letter is somewhere in the Subud Archives.

Is this important? Well in my opinion, yes. Firstly, because Bapak himself chose to make it public. Secondly because Bennett, who had played such a large part in the spread of Subud in the early days, went through a period of doubt and returned to his old habits of 'The Search for the Truth'. However, as he neared the end of his earthly life saw that the Truth had been present all the time within him and sought to acknowledge it. This is something of real importance, especially to those whom he has influenced in the past and who trusted him.

I remember the dream that I had about Bennett shortly after the time he gave in his Helper's card and left Subud. In the dream I was following a pattern that I had done often in the past. I was going up the stairs of Coombe Springs to his vast study where the young people's group used to meet early in the morning before breakfast and going off to work. I went to ask for advice. He looked at me and said, "Do you not know I know absolutely nothing?"

There are moments in my life now when I could say the same. It is not negative, in fact just the opposite. "God only knows" is an expression not often used these days, but it is full of truth. Socrates famously used to bring people to the point of admitting their own ignorance, the point of departure for beginning to understand something. Bennett himself talked about Knowledge, Being, and Understanding.

I know that I need to make continuous efforts to engage in life. But I also know for sure, that whether or not I am truly happy does not depend on the efforts I make. It depends on being aware of the Grace that encompasses us all and feeling the gratitude for that Grace.

Bapak's First Heart Attack

It is back again in 1972 and Rohana receives an urgent call from Bapak's house for me to come immediately. I am out on a call but as soon as I reach my clinic I rush back to Wisma Subud and to the big house.

Bapak is lying on his back in bed saying he is feeling a little tired and he has an ache in his left shoulder blade. He is entirely relaxed, and just a little curious about what is happening to him. Sitting, lying down, walking, he always has this magnificent self-assured dignity about him.

I do a physical check and find his pulse is fast, with an occasional dropped beat. His blood pressure is on the low side of normal. It happened that I had just purchased an electrocardiograph for my practice, I sped to the clinic and came straight back and did an ECG. I was amazed to see the raised ST segments across all the chest leads, which indicated infarction of the heart muscle.

I rang my colleague at the American Embassy, Dr Art Hegelstein. He had retired after many years as a cardiologist, and had chosen to have some years abroad as an Embassy physician. A delightful fellow, and like me, just trying to learn the piano in his spare time. When I showed the ECG to him, he went quiet and said to me "How is this person alive? The whole of the anterior (front) wall of the left ventricle is infarcted" (infarction is when the muscle begins to die after its blood supply is cut off).

I returned to Bapak's bedside and told him what I had heard and said to him, "You know Bapak that I am just a GP. You need to be in hospital under the care of a specialist cardiologist".

He answered and said, "No. You will receive what to do for me and I will follow your treatment. Besides which, don't worry, the Angels are my specialists". As I type the words to this memory I half laugh, half cry, half just choke up. Just such incredible Faith in the Power of God to protect him and his Mission, and such wonderful humility.

I checked with Art Hegelstein daily with my management plan and indeed tried to receive what to do. I was on high-octane energy. I simply did not believe that Bapak would die then.

The question often asked is "Why did a Messenger of God not look after his body?" He smoked. He was over-weight. He did not take enough exercise and he drank quantities of Coca Cola, a drink full of raw sugar. Well I cannot answer that question, except to say that Bapak pushed himself to pass on to all Mankind this Gift of the Spiritual receiving of Subud, which he had received. Often he did not spare himself. In those days, the side effects of smoking were not well known, or the effects of too much sugar on the body's metabolism. Bapak never said he understood and knew everything, although we, in our awe and admiration of him, might often have assumed so.

These are treasured moments in my life.

The Kilt

Of the many onion layers that form our Self, as we know ourselves, there is the National self. Sometimes it likes to be clearly known by the clothes it wears, the manner and accent of its speech, and sometimes it prefers to be more hidden.

Bapak arranged a party for us all to come to in his home in Wisma Subud and asked us to wear our national dress. I borrowed my bank manager's kilt (how Scots can you be?) and went with Rohana who had also got some tartan attire.

We both performed 'Over the Sea to Skye.'

I noticed that my kilt made me feel like a warrior chief and that I was unable to get to my knees in front of Bapak (as was the Indonesian custom) which normally I felt comfortable doing.

Eventually I found that there is something in my onion layers self that is more loyal to the family of Man (One Mankind) and takes precedence over my loyalty to Queen and country. However, my nationalist feeling is quite strong when I am in Scotland, or even, as I discovered, when I wear Scottish national dress.

As Bapak would often ask, "Do we wear our clothes or do they wear us?"

Rohana and Rachman in Scottish dress at
Bapak's party in Wisma Subud

White Man Brown Man

My parent's generation was very racially prejudiced and I became aware that it had unconsciously invaded my psyche. In order to become clear about this, certain experiences happened to me in my life. It is difficult to change, really change, not just in one's mind and become cosmopolitan, but to realise that I am just one of the nine billion of us.

In 1934 I was born in a Forest Officer's bungalow in Coorg India, at the tail end of the British Raj. It was in the jungle in the monsoons, and my mother said the sun came out for a moment at my birth. The midwife of course was Indian. Born with me, I suspect, was the feeling of supremacy of the white, British, Christian culture over the brown masses, and that it was our duty to care for them and educate them. Tolstoy wondered how 150,000 rather stupid Brits could govern 500 million rather intelligent Indians.

In 1968 I was living in Wisma Subud in Jakarta with my wife Rohana, who was pregnant, and our four children aged seven to two. We lived in a very basic way, with no modern conveniences. We were on an Inner adventure of spiritual awakening and development and an Outer adventure to a new culture. This was the ancient proud culture of Java that had been colonised by Westerners for over three centuries, leaving scars on the national psyche. It was a real challenge for my understanding. I began a love/hate relationship with Indonesia.

I loved the intuitive feeling of the Javanese, their inbred sensitivity to others, their humour, their ability to share and help one another, especially amongst the poor. I hated the injustices, the greed, the domination by the powerful, the addiction to hubris and the jealousy and envy. This was the other side of the coin to their sensitivity.

One night I had a dream where I saw some of our future grandchildren. They had slightly brown skins, in fact a golden brown.

Within 10 to 15 kilometres of us was another white person, a young American woman from the middle class of the Middle West. She also was in rebellion to her respectable middle class roots, with a deep thirst for the romance of a completely different culture. She first married an African student whom she met at University and then, when he left her after two years to go as a scholar to Harvard, she married an Indonesian student. They went to live in Indonesia, taking her son by her first marriage with her. His name was Barak Obama.

From the start she plunged into the culture with a passionate desire to help the poor. She worked in programs to alleviate poverty which were funded by foreign aid organizations. She still had time to see that her son learnt how to write and speak good English, prodding him first thing in the morning to complete his assignments. She also took him outside at night to look at the stars, to wonder at the magnificence, the immensity and the beauty of the night sky. Six years later she sent him back to her parents in Hawaii, the place of her University, to be educated. His grandmother went back to work to earn the fees for a good private school. She went on with her work in Indonesia and died an early death from cancer. One of my patients knew her well. Her son went on and later wrote the story of his own search for identity in a cool, intelligent, self-questioning manner in an autobiography called 'Dreams of my Father.' Later, of course, he was elected President of the USA.

My material circumstances improved and within two years I had a medical practice that included 162 companies and institutions, amongst which were almost all the aid organizations and government advisers. It was fascinating to be in the middle of developing history, albeit with its consequent hubris.

I had however a feeling of perpetual discomfort with the increasing disparity between the rich and the poor. I was fortunate to meet and become friends with a Catholic friar and a nun. A number of my friends gathered around these two and we formed a Foundation to work with the poor. Most of my spare time was spent on this.

After fifteen years my success as a foreign doctor with a large practice (I was only allowed to see expatriates) aroused the jealousy of my Indonesian specialist colleagues. After a few narrow shaves I had ceased using them, and referred my patients to specialists in Singapore instead. Through their influence on government departments, I suddenly received an order to leave the country within 24 hours.

How much was this due to the white supremacy feeling still in me and how much due to their jealousy and envy matters little now, although it was to cause me much-needed suffering. I was to go on and work for five years as a well-paid slave in the golden cage of Saudi Arabia to meet the expenses of my children's education. I was to experience the arrogance of the Brown Arab supremacy for those five years, robbed of my own personal initiative.

But the dream of forty years ago has been fulfilled. Two of our daughters have married brown men and so we do now have six golden brown grandchildren of whom I am exceptionally proud.

Good bye White Man's Burden. Hello to One Mankind.

Travelling With Bapak

In the mid-seventies, I accompanied Bapak on one of his world trips. The party included Ibu Mas Tuti whom Bapak had recently married, Tuti and Muti his granddaughters, and Sharif Horthy and myself.

Our first stop was Tokyo where the Japanese were holding their National Subud Congress. Like all nations and races, the Japanese have a certain exclusiveness built into their culture, based on their history, language and the times when they were isolated from the rest of the world. During the Second World War, Indonesians had suffered terrible privations and humiliations under Japanese occupation, as did Allied prisoners of war whom I had known as a child. So to witness the Japanese members' huge respect, gratitude and love of Bapak, who had personally suffered in the war, was something truly warming.

A lot of thought had gone into making us welcome and they had been very generous in supporting the creation of the latihan hall in Wisma Subud and the various enterprises that Bapak had started. They themselves had started various enterprises and Bapak and his party were taken around them. At the end of the Congress there was a show with various songs and dances. Bapak said that although Japanese culture and language was so different from his own Javanese culture, he could understand and appreciate it because essentially all human culture was One. All human beings were meant to recognise that we were of One Mankind.

"Tomorrow," he said "I will arrive in San Francisco and the American Subud brothers and sisters will waive their hands like this and say, "Hi Bapak!"

The next morning the party were waiting for the plane and Bapak pushed over a biscuit to eat, and I refused saying I was fasting. "There is no need to fast when you are travelling," he said. The next moment we were talking about raising funds to complete the PTS Widjoyo building in Jakarta, by selling the rental space for a 30-year period or longer, to various investors. Up till then it was mostly the wealthy Subud members who had been approached. "Would it be possible," I suggested, "for individuals or groups to purchase a few metres at a time according to their means?"

"Yes, indeed." Bapak answered.

It was a long and tiring journey across the Pacific and when we arrived in San Francisco the welcome by the Americans was exactly as Bapak had mimed. After we reached the home that the group had assigned to Bapak and his party, he sat down, took off his shoes and had a cup of tea. Then went straight down to the National Congress and gave a talk to the four hundred or more people who were there.

Bapak was always willing to put the requirements of his mission above his own personal needs. He drew on his reserves of energy to ensure everything was accomplished, no matter how large or small.

On Elevators, Clothes and the Importance of Being Handsome

I have two special memories, alive and meaningful, which concern Bapak and elevators. For these stories, the American word 'elevator' is more pertinent than the English word 'lift'. One of these special memories includes a nuanced lesson about clothes, and their effect on us.

I accompanied Bapak on his world trip in 1977. It was perhaps a kind of present to me for looking after him with his heart attack and his subsequent attacks of arrhythmia.

He had asked my wife Rohana's permission before hand, and when she assented, asked her whether there was anything she wanted. She replied, "Bapak, Rachman has no care about his appearance at all, please can you help?"

The other people in the party were Ibu Mas Tuti, who was Bapak's new wife, his two granddaughters Tuti and Muti, and Sharif Horthy.

I have never liked clothes shopping. I appear not to have any dress sense, nor did I pay particular attention to my appearance. Other things interested me and I did not see the relevance of looking smart or tidy. My only concern was that my clothes were comfortable. Rohana is the complete opposite and for her looking good is important. I was content to remain ignorant on the subject, despite Sharif handing me a book on how to dress to be successful.

When we were shopping as a group in San Francisco we came to a large men's clothing store and Bapak came in with me and said "Boronglah" which means "Buy up the shop!"

The shop was large with very high ceilings and also very light. For the first time in my life I enjoyed looking around for a lightweight summer suit and found one. It was an off white with a very fine line check pattern on it. I put it on straight away.

About a week or two later we were going up in an elevator in New York and I found Bapak looking at me approvingly and saying something.

"Handsome" Sharif translated to me.

Handsome was a word that mattered perhaps to Bapak. He was fulfilling his mission to hand on and explain the benefit and use of the latihan to the world. But he was also in love with his wife, whom he had just married. This was his third marriage and her second. It was a kind of honeymoon.

The next elevator experience was when we were going up in the Twin Towers, about 200 floors high. Elevatory and elevating. Bapak said, "Many of man's inventions in the material world mirror what is already there in the spiritual world. For instance, this lift is like the Ascension which I experienced."

Later we reached the top of the building and looked across at the other tower. Just a few months before our visit, a Frenchman had managed to sling a wire between the two towers and walk across. We wondered at his courage and ingenuity.

Bapak stood at the top of some stairs with Ibu Mas Tuti beside him. She was maybe twenty years younger than him. It was a moment of real happiness for them, and for me an opportunity to witness the importance of a man being handsome.

On our return to Wisma Subud, Bapak asked Rohana if she was satisfied.

Twilight in Jakarta

It is over 50 years since I first visited this city. Jakarta was to have such an effect on my life and development towards becoming a true human being. Now in my twilight years I reflect back to those times.

Then there were only three buildings above ten stories in height in the city; now there are thousands, reaching ever further out into the countryside, some over 50 stories high. Then the immigration officials scowled at me. Now as I line up for immigration I find a friendly smile, as a young woman in a hijab spots me walking to and fro as I deal with a feeling of faintness I get if I stand too long in a queue. She beckons me forward to the front of the queue! Fifty years ago the lights were dim from scarce electricity but the atmosphere was dark, also, from the fear that had spread through the population after a counter coup from the army had left almost a million dead.

GESTAPU is the acronym for 'gerakan September tiga puluh', meaning the movement of September the 30th. An assassination squad led by a Colonel Untung had murdered six of the seven top army generals. The apparent saviour of the day was General Suharto who was the commander of the reserve army corp. He brought in his troops and surrounded the rebel army officers, talked with them and got them to surrender. It appears now that Colonel Untung had at one time been a close friend of his. However, it did not lead to peace and reconciliation, but to the bloody counter coup and the elevation of the army officers into positions of power and influence.

Many people who had any socialist or communist sympathies had their identity cards stamped with the GESTAPU acronym on them, thus preventing them getting any government or business jobs. GESTAPU took place one year before my first arrival and the atmosphere of danger and fear were well described in the book and film 'A Year of Living Dangerously'.

In my initial time there, the story was simple. The 'baddies' were the communists who had tried to take over the state. The 'goodies' were the army who had restored the Constitution. Even then I had my doubts about the army generals and their abuse of power, which is well illustrated in Barak Obama's autobiography and which influenced his philosophy of life. As a young boy of six he lived only ten kilometres away from us and was the same age as our eldest son.

The latest historical probing from the left side of politics, suggests that actually GESTAPU was the result of a revolt by young officers who wanted more democratic change in the army and society. The suggestion is that Suharto played a double game with both sides, while he gradually took power. 'The Smiling General', as his American biographer called him, became well-liked by the US and investment poured in from there and the West. I was to become the doctor for many of these organisations and companies that moved in. Some merely wanted to follow the gravy train, some were genuinely interested in both the economic and social development of the country.

Whatever way that time is looked at, murder is murder. The consequences of breaking an agreed and natural law can often never be calculated.

I have loved this country of Indonesia so much but have also hated it.

Why did I and do I love this country? Many reasons:

119

I learnt to hear the murmurings and indications of my heart rather than the ceaseless chatter of my brain.

I saw the smiles and heard the laughter of the poorer people of society who faced the difficulties of their life with such courage and dignity, and yes, happiness.

I liked to see their closeness and the feeling they had for one another, such as the gotong royong tradition in which neighbours help one another.

I liked to hear the call to prayer which marks the passing of the day, and reminds us of an Eternal Power that enfolds us all and all our fellow creatures.

I hated it for the abuse of power, which I was to see exercised frequently by those that had it.

The title of this piece of writing is a novel written by Muchtar Lubis, which illustrates this abuse of power. The novel describes life in Jakarta in the late fifties. The characters include two betjak drivers who just manage to glean a living. It includes also a mealy mouthed editor of a leading newspaper who boot licks the regime. There is also a bored young man who does not know what to do with his life and many other characters.

Muchtar was a fighter and a writer who knew the power of the pen and who was not afraid to use it to expose corruption in high places. He was also a friend of a mutual friend and Subud member who was also fighter writer, Varindra Tarzie Vittachi. President Sukarno (and later President Suharto) warned Muchtar that if he continued to write in this way he would be jailed. He was jailed and took the opportunity to read widely and deeply.

I liked the book, which became a kind of prelude to some of the work that I would eventually get into with the poor in Jakarta. I said to myself "I would really like to meet this man".

My wish was fulfilled in an interesting, serendipitous way. About one to two years after we had begun to live in Jakarta when everyone was poor, including ourselves, and the children were suffering from the aftermath of whooping cough, we decided to take a holiday up in the hills above Bogor. We hired a cottage looking out over the paddy fields and the mountains in the distance. The children went out on ponies and had their adventures. We inhaled not only the fresh air but also the beauty of the place.

Our old Fiat broke down, there were few cars then that were newer than twenty years old. I managed to get it to the car mechanic at the bottom of our dusty pebbled road. After his repairs he proposed we take a trial ride up to the top of Puncak Pass. We did, and at the top the car broke down again. He suggested I try and hitch a ride down the hill while he fiddled with the car so he could later take it down to his garage.

I stood on the edge of the road with my thumb in the air, remembering my student days. After a lot of cars passed by, a man in a huge old American jalopy stopped, and offered me a lift. The English of the driver was not fluent but we soon got talking and engaged in interesting conversation as we wound our way around all the curves of the road around the tea plantations.

As we stopped at my destination I introduced myself, and he answered, "I am Muchtar Lubis".

We met again from time to time as I read his articles in Newsweek and he visited me to ask me to write an article on Jamu, the local herbal medicines, which were sold in the market and by local women vendors.

There is a saying in Indonesian. "Orang lurus, orang kurus". Meaning an honest straight man is a thin one. He had not lined his pockets with ill-gotten gain. Muchtar was tall, thin and straight.

Through the years I experienced a nauseous feeling whenever I read the editorial of the Jakarta daily. I knew the name of the Editor and owner and I asked Muchtar as he sat beside me on our sofa, on one visit to our house, if his newspaper editor character in his novel was modelled on this man? He turned to me and smiled at me. "How did you know that?" he said.

Adaptation to the
World After Indonesia

The Higher Self

Outside the sun beats down on the porta cabin, one of many grouped together for the workers building a new city in the north-eastern part of the Saudi Arabian desert. They house the many different nationalities who come here to work in order to support their families in their own countries.

It is a lonely and hard life. Many have to work in temperatures up to fifty degrees centigrade. They are mostly Koreans, Filipinos, Indians and Pakistanis with a sprinkling of other Arabs such as Palestinians, Lebanese and Yemenis. They are brought in at midday for lunch but all they want is to lie down after swallowing their meal in about three minutes. Most of them suffer indigestion.

The desert extends far into the distance. Gunfire is occasionally heard when the wind blows from the north. It is Iraqis firing on Iranians. A bloody and useless war, but is the reason for all those building this military city. Its purpose is to guard against that crazy Saddam Hussein, who may want to impose his idea of how Arab society should be onto the Kingdom of Saudi Arabia. This city is called King Khalid Military City.

The desert, although sparse of any vegetation, does hold some inhabitants. These are the Bedouin. They may appear poor and lowly but they certainly do not bear themselves like that. Their homes are made of goat hair and give good shade, strung from a straight horizontal bar about a metre and a quarter up, and extending back to enclose a carpet, bedding rolls and cooking utensils. Nothing much has changed since the Prophet Abraham wandered through here some 4 to 5 thousand years ago, except for a gas bottle and a pick-up truck.

They occasionally bring their children to the medical clinic where the first priority is a complete scrub down, to remove every possible kind of pathogen, before a doctor sees them.

The social life of staff and workers is limited mainly to conversation at meal times, which in the evenings may extend for a few hours, where stories and jokes are exchanged.

I am one of the doctors and one Friday I am sitting on the bed in my porta cabin. I am feeling sorry for myself and bemoaning my fate. Two years ago I was leading a fulfilling life. Medical Director of a large clinic in Jakarta looking after 165 different companies and organizations with a reputation as a reliable and trustworthy doctor. I was physician to my spiritual guide. I was Vice-Chair of a Yayasan (Foundation) for the poor and street people of Jakarta, working with a Dutch friar, a nun and a group of friends with different skills. I had my own home with wife and children around me. I thought I was happy. In fact, I am sure I was happy, although I lived with a sword of Damocles hanging over me. I knew that I could be sent out of the country at any time for offending the sensibilities of my Indonesian specialist colleagues, to whom I no longer referred patients. Then the sword fell. I was given twenty-four hours to leave Indonesia. My family of six children still needed to be educated and looked after - hence my presence in this desert outpost.

As I sat there I noticed something happening to me in my solar plexus. A slow vibration moving backwards and forwards in the pit of my stomach, moving to my chest. This vibration was accompanied by a silence, which became deeper and deeper as it penetrated my whole being, cleansing all feeling of self-pity and the thoughts that accompanied it. Slowly this sacred silence expanded, as it deepened and included my chest and then my head and brain. It then moved further out until I felt surrounded by a large Being.

This Being knew everything about me, my faults, my mistakes, my arrogance in pretending to know and understand what I did not, my fears, my cowardice, my foolhardiness. Despite all this, this Being loved me with a depth and width that I had no knowledge of before. Moreover, I knew that this Being had always been there, beside me, above me, below me, all my life and before.

So who was He, She, It? The question hung there. My spiritual guide Muhammad Subuh? No.

Jesus Christ? No.

My own soul, my own Higher Self? Yes, probably.

I then remembered what Bapak had said to Rohana and me, as we gathered together in his study, before we left our home in Wisma Subud in 1982.

To Rohana who was grieving about leaving Bapak's home and his protection he said, "This is your home and you will return."

To me he said, "You can do latihan at the North Pole or the South Pole or anywhere in the world."

At last, in this isolated desert outpost, I was coming to understand the full meaning of what Bapak had said to me.

Such experiences come to people. It does not change them in a flash; it marks a passage in life, a newer reality, as a more authentic version of themselves emerges. Living with everything you want is OK. But living without everything you want, is also OK.

Maybe the awareness and guidance of one's own soul, which just arises or descends on a person out of the blue, is the most OK of all.

Umra

Working in Saudi Arabia gave me the opportunity to fulfil, in part, the fifth obligation of any Muslim, to make the pilgrimage to Mecca.

I had become somewhat disenchanted with Islam as practised in Saudi, by the narrow views of the Saudis who were my employers, and the state compulsion to follow the five daily prayers. The Prophet Muhammad had stated clearly "There is no compulsion in religion".

I disliked the way people of a lower social status were treated. I often listened to the sad stories of Indonesian maids, who we met in the super markets, of how they were trapped and abused by their employers. The disrespect for foreign women, and my wife, particularly upset me. There was little evidence that those higher ideals in Islam of Generosity, Compassion Forgiveness and Understanding, were being practiced. I seemed to feel only the arrogance of newly acquired wealth and the fear and greed it engendered.

Most people who worked for them did so because they had to and were afraid of losing their jobs. I myself refused to listen to the inner promptings to get out of the country and stand more on my own two feet, as regards earning a living to keep 6 children in school or university. I failed to exercise my initiative and felt trapped by my circumstances. Eventually, after five years in Saudi Arabia, I went to Yemen. There, I could again exert my initiative to benefit both my fellow human beings and myself. So my views are somewhat skewed by my own failure to follow my inner promptings.

However, within this situation there were some enlightening and lighter moments. One of these was my friendship with a Somali interpreter Muhammad Nur. We went on walks together on Fridays in the surrounding wadis of Taif, a mountain town about 1500 metres above sea level at the northern end of the Hejaz mountain range. He once explained that it was impossible to translate the word Rachman, since it was something throughout the whole Universe. He gave me the two volumes of the Quran, which are now well worn. He also brought a book he had seen translated by Muhtar Holland, titled 'Inner Islam', which mentioned my name in the preface.

Another friend of mine Basil, an Iraqi doctor, asked me to accompany him to Mecca on Umra. This is the short, one-day pilgrimage. Mecca is a city I usually went through, rather than to, on my way to Jeddah for latihan with a Filipino Subud brother. It was quicker than going on the long desert road via the Christian by-pass.

I had once been to Mecca to visit the Aunt of an old Indonesian friend of mine. She had married another Indonesian when on Haj with her father, many years previously. She lived in the Indonesian quarter of Mecca. Many Muslim nations congregate to live in their own district in Mecca. Her children, all looking Indonesian, could speak only Arabic.

So my Umra was not preceded by any high expectations. Rather, I had the feeling that I would do it since it is required of me.

We made our visit on or around the 25th day of Ramadhan. It was extremely hot. We arrived at about three in the afternoon and parked within walking distance to the huge Haram mosque. Immediately we entered there was a change in my state and attitude. I was no longer under the law, hierarchy and culture of the Saudi state. This was the place open and free for all Muslims, a kind of international zone, where only the law of the Almighty was to be obeyed.

We started by running between the mounds of Marwa and Sarwa the two little hills where the mother of Ishmael had run looking for water until the miracle of the Spring of Zam Zam was found. It was quite tiring in the heat and at the end of a day of fasting. We then ascended to the second floor of the Haram mosque, the tall pillars completely dwarfing us, to say the four rakas of the afternoon prayer. I was usually among the tallest people, but here next to me was a huge Nubian, towering over me, saying his prayers.

We went down to do the ritual circuit around the Kabba, joining a continual moving stream of humanity walking anticlockwise. This movement is in synchrony with the turning of our planet Earth, that produces our Days and Nights. It is so often quoted in the Quran as one of the signs of Allah and his Compassion for Mankind. It also suggests the balance of work in the day and inner reflection by night.

My ribs were being bruised by the elbows of my fellow pilgrims, white, pink, yellow, black, brown and every hue between. Pilgrims rich and pilgrims poor, young and old, healthy and the sick being carried on stretchers. We were all One humanity. Some of my British superiority and arrogance, born at the tail end of the Empire, was beginning to be stripped away, as I experienced a new relatedness to all mankind. After this we returned to the Haram mosque to await the Margrib prayer. Although this was 35 years ago, I can remember us lined up in circles around the distant Kabba, in gradually descending rows.

After the prayers we realised we had left our food in the car, but all our neighbours shared their meal with us. Someone came around and gave us a handful of dates and we slaked our thirst from the Zam Zam water held in red plastic containers at the end of each row.

I was in a state of elation. A certain grace had arisen in me and something that needed to be cleaned had been cleansed. This was an experience never to be forgotten.

Dreams, Death and Redemption

In the mid-1980s I was living in the hill town of Taif in Saudi Arabia. One night, when I hadn't done latihan for two weeks, I dreamt I was dead, quite dead and in my grave. It was truly horrible in every sense of the word and it woke me up and I was led into our sitting room where I immediately went into latihan and travelled from this state of hell to a very blissful state of heaven.

I then laid down on the couch where I had another dream.

In this dream I was sitting with my old friend Lambert Gibbs on a bench somewhere, side by side with our arms around each other's shoulders. We were chatting and laughing together. Suddenly I turned to him and said "How come you are here chatting with me, when you died last year?"

At that moment I awoke with a shock my hairs standing up on the back of my neck. Lambert and I had always been close; we could say things to one another that we could not with others.

About a year before he died I had stayed in his house in London and felt very uncomfortable. I got up in the middle of the night to latihan and find out what to do. I walked into his sitting room and found him sitting there. I asked him whether he would like me to leave and he said yes. I moved out the next morning. He was under a lot of stress and like many who are very creative could be quite paranoid. He thought that I was making out with Maria his wife.

Later, knowing that I loved the music of Bach which he could play spontaneously, he gave me a little 3 volume 'Introduction to the Performance of Bach' by Rosalyn Tureck. Written on the inside of the first volume is:

For Abdurrachman from Lambert as a token of 30 years of friendship and transgression for which I ask to be forgiven.
October 1983

Of course I am crying as I write this and reflect on the importance of this process of seeking forgiveness before I die.

May Lambert indeed be forgiven his transgressions and rewarded for all his many good deeds in his life.

It is OK to be Angry

I admire real warriors. My father was one, but I know I am a pacifist. I know the cost of suffering and the misery of war. But one day I discovered that it is OK to be angry, in fact not just OK, but really good. It is OK to fight for one's rights as a human being.

I had been working in Saudi Arabia for five years to meet the needs of my children at school or university. Sometimes I said to myself that one simply has to live outside one's comfort zone to meet the responsibilities of one's life.

However, I hated that society, and did not know quite how much, until my last day in it.

I hated it for its attitude to women particularly foreign women. I hated it for its hypocrisy which oozed out of the seams and interstices of the state, its arrogance, its lack of real empathy and its prescriptive interpretation of Islam. I hated it for the atmosphere of fear that was everywhere, the fear of losing one's job.

It took me a long time to acknowledge the truth that living there was bad for me. It was also bad for my family for whom I was sacrificing my time in this hostile environment. It took me time to look for other ways to fulfil my responsibilities.

Among other indignities for those working there, was the removal of our passports by the personnel office. Each of us was nervous when we went to the personnel office to see if our visa to leave the country was ready.

On asking for my exit visa in my passport, I was told to wait by some young Saudi bedouin, while his mates ate their breakfast with their feet up on the desk. Our flight was booked for the next day.

While I was sitting, a nervous, pretty young nurse came in and asked the same question. The young bedouin men leered at her. I noticed that something was happening to me, as if my head was a boiling kettle and the top of my skull was the lid lifting up and down. Eventually the young guy who had gone off to enquire about my visa returned and said it was not ready.

I was really quite surprised at what happened next. I suddenly pounded the table and shouted at the top of my voice, "Why not?"

Suddenly lots of men came running out of their offices including the head of the personnel department, wanting to know why the normally quiet and peaceful Dr Rachman was angry. The head of the department assured me that the exit visa would be waiting for us at the airport the next day. My anger had had productive, practical results - an exit visa on time!

But more important was the sense of liberation when the feeling, the words and the action are totally at one. It is more than OK to be angry, it is absolutely right.

The Road by the Queen of Sheba's Palace

"How about danger money?" I asked, feeling maybe that I had sold myself a little short in my modest salary request, and knowing that Yemenis were on the wild side and free with the use of the gun.

"Oh! Don't worry about that. The worst that can happen to you, is for your back tyres to be shot out".

My interviewer was an attractive, blonde Texan millionairess, and the interview took place in a plush, 5 star Kensington Hotel suite in early 1987. It was for the position of Medical Director of Yemen Hunt Oil Company.

I sensed she was not telling the truth, but I did not care, as I really wanted the job, after five years of a very sterile, constrained life in Saudi Arabia. I had been working in a 'golden cage' to get my children through University. All my initiative then had to be set aside to simply work in a pigeonhole, as I was directed. I wanted a job where I could use my initiative again, to be able also, in some way, to serve the poorer sections of the community. I also wanted some adventure, some risk, some real responsibility and challenge. This was the introduction to my 1001 days and nights in Al Yemen, Arabia Felix.

Yemen lies at the south of the large Arabia Peninsula with a population of over 20 million. The end of a long mountain range, the Hijaz, runs down the middle, thus creating sections occupied by slightly different groups of people: the hill tribes of the mountains, the people of the plains whose appearance reflects the African influence from across the Red Sea, and on the other side of those 10,000-foot-high mountains are the Bedouin of the desert regions.

My first day at work confirmed what I had sensed in the interview. A pickup was parked near my new clinic in Sana'a, the capital of North Yemen. There was a bullet hole in the rear window just 4 inches to right of the driver's neck and the bullet was buried in the doorframe. It was twilight and the driver did not see the group of Bedouin telling him to stop. They opened fire. He was checked out at the clinic. He then treated himself to two double whiskies and caught the next plane back to the UK, never to return.

One of the tasks of my new job was to go to the CPU (Central Processing Unit) for three or four days each month, to see patients, supervise the work of the paramedics and do inspections with the safety officer. It was a fairly large camp, housing 350 men in porta cabins. The CPU itself was for processing the crude oil, so it could flow along a pipeline 400 kilometres to the sea. It went over a 3000-metre range of mountains and so had pump stations, which I also visited.

The CPU itself lies just 40 kilometres north of what used to be the Queen of Sheba's palace. It is as if her mythical buried treasure has now been found and is to be used, thirty centuries later, for the benefit of all her people.

The journey from Sana'a to the CPU takes about three hours. We pass through two long valleys separated by two escarpments and gorges and then come to the sands of the Empty Quarter on our left, and some rocky hills and scrub on the right. Young shepherds guard their sheep with an AK 47 cradled in their arms. The local Bedouin had hijacked about fifteen of the company's Land cruisers, so now we are instructed always to take a Bedouin driver. He has a Kalashnikov by his side, and being fairly poor, the barrel and the stock are often held together with sticking plaster. No Bedouin will risk a tribal war by killing another Bedouin.'

We eventually reach the little town of Marib and then continue on till we pass the Queen of Sheba's palace. Bilquis was her real name and I will come to her story later. She has been celebrated in opera, in the Bible, and the Quran, but more importantly she lives on in the hearts of most Yemenis, who often name their daughters after her.

All that remains of her palace are 8 stone pillars standing five metres high with another 4 shorter pillars in the desert sand. Each pillar consists of five blocks of stone standing on top of one another, the interstices hardly seen, such was the accurate cutting of the stones. There have been many archaeological digs over the last 100 years. In the last 30 years, modern technology has discovered a vast area that was a palace and also the remains of a great city. We know that there was a state called Saba with possibly as many as a million and a half citizens, and this was a great civilisation. The huge Marib Dam irrigated a sufficient area to grow food to support such a large population. Fifteen hundred years ago there was a civil war, the dam was not looked after and slowly it silted up. The people dispersed, leaving what is now a tiny village. However, one of the descendants of the old Saba is the Emir of Abu Dhabi. Forty years ago he gave 65 million dollars to make a new dam and the area is slowly coming alive again.

Those eight pillars, which I passed so often, caught my imagination. Archaeologists dispute whether they were part of temples to the Sun or the Moon. But the story from the Quran is as follows.

The Prophet Suleiman (or Soloman in the Old Testament) enquires somewhat angrily where the Hoopoe is. This queen of the birds is his chief spy. Suleiman has been given the power to converse with both animals and the spirits. Eventually the Hoopoe turns up to tell him she has seen a Queen of remarkable intelligence and beauty, who dwells in the powerful state of Saba. She has a great throne inlaid with gold and precious stones. But she worships the Sun and not the Lord of the Universe.

Suleiman, who already has a great reputation for wisdom, sends her an invitation to visit him. She discusses whether to accept or not with her counsellors. They advise her to go to war and conquer him. She replies that war leads to killing and the waste of lives. She decides to accept the invitation, against the advice of her counsellors.

Suleiman besides having the power of understanding the language of animals is also able to converse with and have power over the Jinn or spirits. One of these offers to bring the throne of Bilquis to him.

He also has the area in front of his own throne polished so it is as bright as a mirror. When she arrives she thinks she is walking over water and so lifts her skirt to expose her delightful legs. Suleiman beckons to her to come up and sit on the throne beside him and says "Do you like it? I believe it is quite like yours!" They test one another with riddles. She is converted to Islam[10] and they become a couple. The outcome of their relationship is a son called Menyelek, which means "a gift from me to you". He later becomes Emperor of both Saba and Ethiopia. For the next 3000 years many Ethiopian Emperors have been called by that name, and with the title 'Lion of Judah' after their ancestor Suleiman.

---

[10] Muslims understand that the belief in One God began with the prophet Abraham and that all the Jewish prophets are seen as Muslims.

What impresses me is that Bilquis, an unmarried single mother, keeps her throne and her reputation for wisdom. She must have had an extraordinarily strong and self-possessed character.

Of course there is no proof of all this, but it is a story that is believed by most Yemenis (Muslims) and Ethiopians (Christians). Part of it was related to us by an Ethiopian patient who took us out to a dinner of Ethiopian food, with a reminder that we had to be out by 10 pm when the place was turned into a brothel.

My 1001 days and nights in Arabia Felix (Happy Arabia) are brought to an end by the Desert War. Saddam Hussein was in town in June and suddenly General Schwarzkopf is in town in August, just as Saddam's tanks are rolling into Kuwait. I am invited to have breakfast with Schwarzkopf's aide de camp in a move to support the Rehab Unit I visit each week. Unfortunately, the sympathies of many Yemenis lie with Saddam and the atmosphere is considered too risky for expatriate families in the company to remain. I decide to downgrade myself to a fly in fly out doctor, in preparation to settling into work in New Zealand.

On my last journey from the CPU to Sana'a I ask my driver "Whose side are you on, Saddam's or King Abdullah?" (Saudi). "Neither," he says, and tilts his head to the Queen of Sheba's Palace. "She's our Queen".

Infinity and Eternity

To me it is not strange that some of the great revelations and inspirations for Mankind have come from those who have spent time in the vastness, loneliness and hardships of the desert. One night before sleeping, I step out of my porta cabin to take a breath of fresh air. A soft warm wind blows on my face and I hear the sound of birds flying nearby. Great migrations of birds cross here in Yemen each year. There is no moon only starlight.

Moonlight has a deep effect on the inner feeling of a man. It makes him conscious of his longing for a woman to be his partner, and to the creation and continuation of his own line. There are many poems and songs to Moonlight. But Moonlight is only a reflection of the light of the Sun, a reminder our life here is but a shadow of the Great Reality, a Dream, a shadow like Plato's cave or the performance of a Shadow play. It does not emanate of itself.

Starlight is different. I am seeing by the light of billions of suns emanating light from millions of light years away. I sense the number of suns out there must be more than the grains of sand in this vast desert. A stillness and feeling of awe descends on me as my arms rise spontaneously above my head and I am made to bow down before the majesty, the immensity, the glory of it all. I am absolutely nothing in front of all this and yet it encompasses me and connects me to it. Indeed, to Infinity and Eternity.

Experiencing the Zikr

A beautiful recitative on the Oudh floats out the window of a Yemeni house surrounding the tennis courts of the British Embassy Club in Sana'a where I am playing my last game of the day.

Something is about to happen to me of some significance and it starts as a niggle of discomfort and pain in my stomach, which I put down to a big meal followed by a hard game of tennis. I go home to rest and receive a call to visit a German visitor who won't see a local GP. I diagnose appendicitis and call the surgeon and send him into hospital.

Through the night my pain worsens and I get little sleep. I wonder about transference.

In the morning the Yemeni surgeon rings to tell me that my diagnosis was right and that the patient is doing well. I mention that I think I have the same thing, but he is tired and tells me to take some pills. My temperature and pulse are up and I decide to take a car 200K south, where a Dutch surgeon friend of mine runs a hospital for local tribesmen in Dammar.

He keeps 10 beds aside for shotgun wounds. The shooter or his tribe pays for the bed of the guy that has been shot. The economics of this arrangement tends to reduce the rates of injury and encourage negotiation between tribes.

On arrival the diagnosis of appendicitis is quickly made and proven when a huge gangrenous appendix bursts as it is removed. I am given the best room in the hospital and my own toilet. This VIP privilege consists of a hole in the floor, difficult to negotiate while squatting with a drip in one arm and a septic gash in the right side of my abdomen.

The Indian nurse stays with me 24 hours, sleeping with her head on her arms, which rests on the side of my bed. I am touched and grateful for her devotion but the fluid balance chart is not very accurate. I feel I am going down-hill getting more and more ill. I see these great monsters flying at me like in a scene from Jurassic Park. I am not sure whether this is due to my illness or the metronidazole that I am taking. I say to myself, "Rachman, dying is no big problem. Just surrender yourself!" But out of the depths of me comes a far more authentic voice, "What bloody rubbish! You have free choice".

I pick up the phone and ring the company and ask to be transferred to Guys, my old teaching hospital in London. A first class flight is arranged for me on Air France, and a paramedic is sent with me to keep the IV drip going. He is taken up with the gourmet food, the wine and the scented smell of soignée women. He forgets the drip, which stops. When an ambulance at the airport meets us he reluctantly asks whether he should accompany me to the hospital. I tell him to go home.

At Guys I am diagnosed with severe dehydration, peritonitis, pneumonia and wound abscess.

My eldest daughter Lorna meets me there, (Rohana is in New Zealand visiting her mother) and advises me to take a bed in the public ward. She has recently got her Anthropology degree and is keen on the idea of Self Development. "You will learn more there

Dad," she says. Being on the other side of the counter is indeed a very revealing experience.

The surgical registrar is confident and competent and orders a drip, a suck regime that goes on for two weeks, with daily dressings to foul e coli pus, which is pouring out of my belly. I am utterly dependent on the good will of the nurses for my wound toilet. Their good will, of course, ranges from none at all to lots, with mainly the foreign nurses being most helpful.

I recognise the surgical consultant, Sir Somebody or other, from my student days when he was a junior registrar. He does not recognise me. He seems to me to be somewhat inebriated with his exalted position in life, but maybe my view is a little skewed, lying there a smelly mess with all kinds of tubes going in and out of me.

At 2 am each morning I am woken by a 'something' inside that tells me to take a walk. It is as if my legs are moved by themselves and my right hand also as it reaches for the mobile drip stand and I am walked to the corridor outside the ward, and there the sense of the zikr arises spontaneously in my legs, and in fact in my whole body, as this 'something' makes me walk for a half hour or so. The feeling of bliss permeates my whole body. I feel light and very happy.

After 12 days I am allowed something to drink and it goes down. Being witness to the sufferings of others who are my fellow patients, puts my own situation into perspective. Many have terminal illnesses and I can feel their fear. This is brought home to me when I am woken at night sometimes by a series of enormous farts, like a roll of thunder ending with an "Oh my God!" at the end.

On return home I take a 500 metre walk and then sleep for 4 hours, and each day the walk gets longer and the sleep less. I am back at work after just 6 weeks off. My friend, who heads UNICEF in

Yemen, had appendicitis with just wound abscess and was off for three months.

Such experiences as these are like a Rubicon which, once crossed, one never needs to cross again. I was unaware then that I could experience such happiness and joy in the midst of quite severe illness. Thanks indeed to the Grace of the Almighty, which is within and surrounds us all.

Heart Being in the Right Place

When we want to get something done we work at it and plan it. But sometimes there is an element of luck. What brings this luck? Is it perhaps having our heart in the right place?

In 1989 I was in Yemen working as the Medical Director in an oil company. I was allowed to visit the Rehab Centre in Sana'a once a week to give advice where needed. I grew to admire the courage and optimism with which these guys dealt with their disabilities. Many had lost their legs through mine explosions, others had paraplegia or tetraplegia.

They asked me whether I could help find a place for them to play basketball. I liked their initiative in improving their morale and I started to fund raise to rent a place and make a basketball court. Soon we had a team.

Then the idea arose to go to Stoke Mandeville in Britain for the first of the Para Olympics. My friend Penny, the British Ambassador's wife, helped with raising funds and we found a suitable place for them to train. We needed more money. I had asked many times of my immediate boss whether I could see the CEO of the company I worked for, but had been refused. However, on the 17th day of Ramadan that year, I was given permission to see him.

He was young and new to the job. I walked into his office and sat down in front of his desk which had his files neatly stacked to either side of him, like playing cards. I had not seen him before and did not really know him, so I was trying to find the right way to approach what I wanted to say and how to say it.

I found myself saying this.

"It is the seventeenth day of Ramadan, a time when people following the fast find themselves thinking of the needs of others who are not so well off as we are. I am trying to facilitate a Yemeni team to go the Para Olympics. I think it would do the Company's name a lot of good, in the eyes of the local people and the government, if we could support this."

He sat there for a moment thinking.

"Good idea! We will give $25,000 and we will hold a party for all our contractors and get them to give another $25,000."

I was amazed at his enthusiasm and felt so grateful. But the ball kept rolling.

General Schwartzkopf was in town and his Aide de Camp, a Marine Colonel, phoned me one morning and invited me to have breakfast with him.

"We have a whole lot of sports wheel chairs and other rehab equipment which we were going to give to the Sudanese but they have turned nasty. Would you like them? And by the way I think we can fly those guys to England in our army transport."

The team went. They were successful in getting a bronze medal.

I asked myself how did this all happen? I do not know, but what I did know was that my heart was in its right place. It had moved to its right place.

I had no interest in promoting my own reputation and when the government gave a 'Thank you' to us, I was quite happy for it to be received by my friend, the British Ambassador's wife.

Top – Yemeni government reception expressing thanks
for their team's success in the Para Olympics
Bottom - The Mitchell's home in Sana'a, Yemen

Ask and Ye Shall Receive
Synchronicity and Serendipity

We are standing outside on a friend's porch during a break in our Artist's Way course. Someone says, "I like your green shirt". I like it too, the deep green and the blue stripes remind me of the shop where it was bought, the owner of the shop and her husband, Ronald Lewcock. He was the Professor of Islamic Architecture and a Fellow of Claire Hall, at Cambridge University.

In the book 'One Thousand and One Arabian Nights', each story ends with the line "And thereby hangs another tale." And indeed, this brief conversation reminds me of an intriguing tale.

My mind's eye drifts back twenty-three years to the sitting room in our house in Sana'a where Lydia, one of our daughters, is lying on her stomach turning the pages of a large book titled 'Sana'a - An Arabian Islamic City'. It was edited by R.B. Serjeant and Ronald Lewcock.

Lydia is staying with us on a six-month sabbatical from her Art degree at Kingston University in Surrey. She has been told to hold an exhibition in Sana'a at the end of it. She has decided to make the city of Sana'a itself the thesis for her degree.

She suddenly cries out. "This is an incredible book, I would love to meet the author".

The house we are in is built in Yemeni style, with thick walls of stone blocks to hold another story above it, but also to repel bullets. Sana'a is located at a high elevation and the light is shining through windows which are six thousand feet above sea level. Each window is clear in the lower three quarters and coloured in the upper quarter, with a variety of beautiful geometric patterns. The Yemenis love colour. We sit cross legged on the floor, leaning on cube-shaped cushions, the way the locals do. This room is called a mufraj.

Maria, Lydia's older sister, is also with us. She has come to sample Yemeni life, wander the souks and buy Bedouin jewellery. She spent her gap year in Sri Lanka looking after an orphanage for mentally and physically handicapped children. She has fallen in love with the place, and with Ajit Chanmugan who lives there. They plan to marry.

The following day we are again together in our sitting room. Life passes in a more leisurely pace in Sana'a. The phone rings and a voice says "I am Ronald Lewcock. Can I speak to Maria please? I am a friend of Ajit's mother Carmen and she has asked me to look you up while I am in Yemen."

"You are not THE Ronald Lewcock who has produced or edited 'Sana'a an Arabian Islamic City'?" exclaims Lydia.

"Well yes, I have been involved in producing a book of that name."

"When can you come to supper?"

"Tomorrow evening."

Indeed, a fascinating evening followed, with great insights into the history of the city, which I wanted to know for my own curiosity, but which was far more important for Lydia who needed those details for her degree.

Maria and Ajit married sometime later.

Job's Tomb

On the way back to Sana'a one evening, I see a mosque on the horizon of a mountain ridge on the left of me. The light of the setting sun reflects from its dome. "The tomb of the Prophet Job," my driver says. A strange feeling of connection and sympathy stirs in me and I pick up my bible on returning home to read his story again.

The first test given to him is that all his cattle and possessions are stolen by the Sabeans. The last and perhaps the most difficult test for Job to bear was that his friend, Eliphaz the Temanite, turned against him and told him he was not a true believer. These accounts from the Old Testament may hold some clues to the belief that it is Job's tomb.

Although there are many claims for Job's tomb all over the Middle East, I felt the one identified by my driver may be the right one. Firstly, because the Sabeans' descendants, 3000 years later, still live in this region - and are still experts in the stealing business! Secondly, a Welsh geographer friend of mine was mapping the area and pointed out to me that a village called Teman was just near there. This fact aligns with the story told in the Bible that it was a Temanite (Eliphaz) who abandoned Job, criticising him and leaving him entirely on his own to suffer. Certainly the local people believe this to be Job's Tomb, based on stories passed down through the generations.

The Lord's Prayer

The meaning of prayers can come slowly by frequent practise together with life experiences, fasting and good works. Or it may suddenly come out of the blue, in answer to some question that has arisen out of a difficult and unpleasant situation. The latter was to happen to me at a Subud meeting of several hundred people in Holland.

Bapak's widow, Ibu Mastuti was ill with cancer and I had taken on the responsibility of raising funds for her treatment. I went to several wealthy friends and asked for donations on a monthly basis to pay for treatment, all of whom willingly gave. That is, all except the wealthiest, who had been very generous with his wealth in the past, but on this occasion said to me that "she has plenty of money herself for her own treatment". This somewhat shocked me, as the above statement did not correlate with her mode of life and what I observed. I felt also that it did not accord with the respect that Bapak's widow was due.

I awoke the next morning feeling very sad and confused and said to myself "What should I do?" The words of the Lord's Prayer arose spontaneously in me, without my willing it. The prayer repeated itself three times and each time it had deeper meaning and significance as each word followed the other with utter inner truth and rationality.

At the end, the confusion and sadness had utterly left me, to be replaced by joy and a feeling of forgiveness for myself and for my wealthy friend, and compassion for my fellow human beings. I was later able to relate this experience to him.

I had not said the Lord's Prayer for over thirty years. Now it often comes back to me as I wake from my sleep in the early morning.

Bovinity

The other day I was washing up after breakfast. Come to think of it, it was not the other day but more than twenty years ago. We were living in country New Zealand in a cottage that backed onto a small sliver of meadow between our wooden cottage and a wood or, as they say there, the bush.

My mind was not alert as I was thinking of something or other while washing up but suddenly I became aware there was a cow looking at me over the fence. It took me a little time to realise it was actually trying to catch my attention while I was busy chattering in my mind.

When its bovine eyes had locked onto mine as if to say "Have I got your attention now?" it turned its head to its left and then looked at me again. By this time my mind had ceased chattering to itself and had become curious. I walked out of the cottage, turned and climbed over the style into the small meadow. The cow led me down the fence for about a hundred metres where her calf had got stuck in the fence, unable to free itself, which I did in a moment. Up to that event, I had not realised another being not of our species could ask for help. I have recorded the facts. There are hundreds of accounts of animal intelligence, and people who live close to nature can attest to that.

I have loved cows ever since I was given a milking bucket on my sixth birthday with my name on it and two cows, Sooty and Strawberry, to milk when I came back from school. They were gentle creatures and never kicked as I squeezed their udders with my head pressed up against their bristly sides, and listened to their chewing the cud and the sounds of abdominal rumblings. To this day the sight and smell of cow manure gives me a great sense of closeness to Nature.

There is another side to these wonderful creatures that we depend on so much for our food. They can be quite savage if someone gets between a cow and her calf. This happened to me once as the cows were coming for their afternoon milking. I was charged by a cow up the farm road and escaped by diving through the wood rails of the fence at the side of the track. I have since learnt that more people are killed by cows than bulls.

An Upriver Experience

It has been dark for about half an hour. I am standing with the torch in my hand, in the bows. It is not really strong enough for me to see the way ahead through the reeds on either side of the river. At least the motor at the stern is still chugging away and we are moving forward to our destination. Suddenly there is a clap of thunder and then another, the wind begins to stir the reeds and raindrops gently touch, then drum on my scalp. Lightning flashes show up the river ahead as if it were day. They come every fifteen seconds so I have no need of my torch.

This is Life and I begin to sing some song that connects me, the essential me, and the wild Borneo jungle that is around me. It has been a long day and we have flown across four rivers from Palangkaraya, in an eight seater Cessna, to Tanjung Pinang. The police, as usual, have been over officious and demanded to know why we are here and what we are doing. We are a party of five, all from Britain, on a trip to see the rehabilitation centre for orang utan. This is up river from Tanjung Pinang in the National Park which at the date of this story 1989, was a million acres of primary forest.

Professor Kalgitas, one of the three young women inspired by Professor Leakey to study our nearest primate relatives, is the founder of the centre. The others are Diane Fossey who studied the mountain gorillas in Ruanda, and Jane Goodall who studied the chimpanzees.

In fact, we are late and should have arrived before sundown. The engine had broken down and the captain turned out to be a 14-year-old, who then said "Tidak ada teman Tuan," meaning "I don't have a friend sir". So I told him that if he could keep the motor running I would be his 'friend' and do the steering from the bows.

We arrive at the centre a half hour later. Our wireless message from the police station had either not been sent or had not got through. So we are lucky that her second in command is a kindly Javanese and that I can speak Indonesian. He offers his sitting room floor for us to sleep on. The next morning, we wake up and see the orang utan looking at us through the windows. They are interested in their 'cousins', us human primates.

One of my friends, Sachlan North, has wandered off down a slatted wooden trail made to avoid the swamp. At one point it is broken. A large orang utan grabs him by the hand and won't let him go. He is a patient man but a little unsure of what to do. Eventually the water over the sunken wooden trail moves and a large crocodile paddles away. His 'cousin' then lets him go.

Their rehabilitation back into the forest is not an easy task. Having been near humans for so long, they feel closer to us than to their own species. But when they mix with humans, they are often attacked and killed by them. This is a generational re-adaptation programme costing millions of dollars as the habitat of their wild relatives is gradually reduced by deforestation.

It is a sad fact that the local Dyak people are also losing their own traditional environment to the rapacity of timber companies, even as they receive a temporary income from being employed by them. By capturing baby orang utans to sell as pets to those who live in cities, the impoverished Dyaks earn a far greater income.

Walking through primary forest is a primal experience. There is an immediacy and sharpness to my senses. It is as if I had woken up into being a five-year-old again, with all the freshness and wonder of that time of life. I appreciate again the old Tarzan myth. The forester who accompanies us says that they have documented three thousand species of plants and are still counting, and this is before they have started with the trees.

At the time of writing the National Park is down to a third of its former size. Money, as always, talks, despite the best intentions of certain idealists. A recent BBC journalist reporting on this almost lost her life. She was just saved in time by the intervention of a very proactive British Ambassador, who asked the authorities to send the marines in to get her out.

River journeys are quite magical, especially going up river. There is the feel of the boat as it pushes through the placid water. The quiet throb of the engine in the stern. Then there is the constant changing panorama of the greenery of the river's edge.

I dreamed of such journeys as a child and now our daughter, Lorna with her friend Gaye Thavisin have their own boats, bringing tourism to Central Kalimantan. In doing so they provide an income and support for their employees, their families and the villagers, who take the tourists on trips through the jungle.

Reflections on the Death
of My Sister Roanna

My sister Roanna died in 2016 and three weeks beforehand I broke my hip. Herein lies a story.

There was eight years difference between us and a whole lot of rubbish too. I did not know our father as well as she did, since my parents separated when I was three years old and Roanna eleven. The memories of our experiences with 'Daddy' were one of the ways which brought us together earlier in our lives. She adored him due to the simple fact that he always showed his love and care for her. She told me that after a busy day in his work as a forest officer in the Indian jungle, he would come and be with her. When she was about five years old he took her out to watch an elephant giving birth to its calf.

She appeared to have inherited his characteristics of openness, naturalness, generosity and enjoyment of living and good company. He would occasionally go to excess with alcohol, as did Roanna in adulthood. But in general he worked hard, serving as an officer in, as he put it, "The two greatest institutions that this planet has ever known, the Royal Navy and the British Empire!". He was a happy and contented man.

During World War II we would see him for brief periods when he was on leave. A year after the end of the war we met up in London with him and May, his new wife of four years. It was my twelfth birthday and he loaded me with presents. We had a long lunch at the Cumberland Hotel where he told me about his father, and how proud he was of him having started as a sailor and ending as a captain in the Royal Navy.

As Roanna and I left, we did not know this was the last we would ever see of our father. Nine months later he had a fall in his home in India and died. He had reached the pinnacle of his career in the Indian Forest Service as a Conservator of Forests. Roanna had just passed her physiotherapy degree and was about to fly out to India for a holiday. It seemed to me she weathered her grief and disappointment better than I did.

While Roanna's relationship with our father was so warm and happy, it was the opposite with our mother who constantly criticised her. It is possible my mother's attitude to Roanna was caused by disappointment that she was not a boy. Her first child Jackie, born when she was just twenty, died of diphtheria at the age of eighteen months. Her friend Irene Lowe, who was a school inspector and a Quaker, advised her to have another child soon to fill that empty gap in her life. Irene offered to be the godmother and took her role very seriously especially when our parent's marriage broke up several years later.

So it was to Irene that Roanna went after an angry row with our mother, when she was aged twenty-two. Irene's advice was to see the world and become independent. So very shortly after this meeting, my sister took a physiotherapy post in Malaya. There she learnt to sail, fly, play all sorts of sports and run her own home independently and enjoy life to the full. She later went on to work in New Zealand and Canada.

However, when our mother began to weaken, in the mid nineteen seventies, it was Roanna who went home and built on a flat to our mother's house so that she could look after her. As she had to spend more time as a carer, she had to work part-time as a physio and was retired at half pay when she was sixty. This, together with the delay of the sale of our mother's house, led to quite a long depression with financial hardship. She went to work as a carer in a religious home of healing, Burswood, where she recovered her sense of well-being. Although mentally I recognised that I owed something to Roanna for looking after mother, it did not reach me fully emotionally. I still judged her in a rather superior way, perhaps like my mother.

Her financial situation was helped by a large bequest from her godmother. But, gradually over the last ten years, her financial resources drained and she was forced to mortgage her flat and to live on the capital. At the same time her health and ability to get around began to deteriorate. The slow steps into old age began to take place. First, getting rid of the car, next a stick, then a walker. Then asking taxi drivers to bring her shopping up. Falls out of bed and inability to get up by herself led to calls for the ambulance medics, who would put her back to bed. Next came severe cardiac arrhythmias with a sense of impending death, severe chest pain and rapid heartbeat and admissions to hospital. Investigations revealed that she had a restriction of her aortic valve which lay at the basis of all this.

So started the weekly phone calls then on to daily or even twice daily calls. I would say to myself "patience" each time she called as I knew the next hour would be taken up with listening to a long monologue on her activities for the last 24 hours or so. Neither of us had ever learnt the art of conversation. Her phone calls to me would start with "Hallo Darling," coming from a place in her of true kindred feeling and love for me. My response never measured up to that, through my own emotional ignorance and unawareness. Since a child her behaviour had always embarrassed me. She veered from putting me on a pedestal to then knocking me off with some embarrassing childhood tale.

Her physical condition began to deteriorate quite quickly with more episodes of rapid arrhythmia, breathlessness and chest pain. There were frequent admissions to the local hospital. The cardiologists' opinions were divided. One said she is not fit for a valve replacement to relieve the narrowing of her aortic valve, the other saying she will die sooner if she doesn't have it done. She signed up for a trial of a new prosthesis for her aortic valve in order to get it done. In November she left her flat to go 40 miles away to have the procedure. She was never to return to the home she so loved.

Following the procedure, she was unable to sit up, stand or walk, and her speech became impaired. There was no evidence of a stroke and the physicians did not make a diagnosis, so she was shipped off to rehabilitation, which was unsuccessful. The next six months were to be spent lying on her back. We kept in very close contact by phone with the East Sussex social services and were very lucky to find a very caring, clean and well run nursing home near to Eastbourne, her old home town. She was not initially impressed or pleased with the place but her friends and our children lauded it. She said, "Life is no longer any fun".

I have omitted to say that twenty years earlier she became a Catholic. She repeatedly said the change had made a great difference to her faith in God. I said to myself, "If that is true then you don't need to tell me that so often". I wrote her a letter telling her that grumbling in the Catholic faith is not allowed and the only way for her now, hard as it is, is to accept her situation. I beat myself about the preachy tone of that letter but Lorna our eldest daughter said it really helped her.

At the end of May, I was packing a suitcase for our intended flight to England to be with Roanna when I lost my balance and fell directly and heavily onto my left side. The pain was immediate, as was the realisation that I had broken my hip. Above and beyond the expletives of "Bugger it, bugger it!" arose the question of why did I fall? Just as fast, or even faster, out of the blue came the reply, "Pride comes before a fall". During the next two weeks a series of experiences unfolded which added flesh to the bones of that seemingly trite statement. Within experience - and particularly of the hard and painful sort - there is a lot of learning for the heart.

Some three years ago I had a cardiac procedure which involved cauterising or burning a small part of the inside of my heart. Despite some analgesia, it was painful. However I found that the sensation of physical pain was no different from that of emotional heartache that I had often felt in the past. Following my fall, the ambulance was called and I was speedily relieved of my pain as I was bundled onto a stretcher and into the ambulance by a very competent medic. At Fremantle Hospital Accident and Emergency I joined the queue and the Indian radiographer confirmed my self-diagnosis with a cheerful grin. "Yes, you have a fractured neck of femur. There are 21 others waiting to be done", he said.

My sense of independence gradually moved to dependence on others for everything from relief of bladder and bowels, to relief of pain, to being moved. My pride, if it did not actually fall, inevitably began a slight downward motion. But there was much more learning to come, perhaps of a deeper and more liberating kind. The shock arising from the pain and loss of blood of the fracture brought on atrial fibrillation, with my heart rate going up to treble its normal rate. This reduced the perfusion of my coronary arteries and I began to feel strong pain in my chest as if I was being crushed, at the same time I became short of breath. "Hang on here", I said to myself, "this is very similar to what Roanna has been going through for the last two to three years".

The realisation of this coming from my heart itself produced at the same time, both tears of remorse and a wry chuckle at the Divine Joke that was being played on me. This chest pain had brought me closer to a certain reality, where for a moment, judgement was suspended and only the essence feeling of being a brother mattered.

I was moved to the cardiac ward so that staff could keep an eye on me. Our eldest son came from New Zealand, our eldest daughter from Indonesia and our middle daughter from Malaysia came to visit me, just in case I was on my way out! With their help I managed to phone Roanna and express my true feelings to and for her.

One week later she passed on.

The Music Lesson

He had planned this outing for some time, this seventy-nine-year-old doctor. Can, could, is it possible to lead some of his grandchildren to an appreciation of classical music, the way it had touched and inspired him through moments of crisis in his life?

He is sitting on his porch in the summer sun waiting for them to pick him up. He can no longer drive because of a constricting visual field. He is fussing. Why is she late? The concert starts at 3 pm and it takes 16 minutes at least to get to the Fremantle Town Hall, where the concert is being held.

In the car he parades his knowledge in a somewhat didactic manner. "Do you know who Richard Wagner was? What did Tchaikovsky compose? The Nutcracker suite. Great. What else?" Along he goes in his old fashioned school master 'Stephen Fry' style. He has a feel he is not engaging and his erudition is like water flowing off a duck's back, but still it is nice to be with these three young women. Two are about to go to University, the other has two more years at school.

At the square outside the fine Edwardian Town Hall, with its nice clock tower, people queue for tickets. The concert cannot start until they are all through. Two members from his writing group of three years ago come up and are introduced to his young companions. He wonders what they make of his friends but does not ask.

Soon they are seated in the upper gallery of the town hall, looking down on the stage as the members of the orchestra gather and settle themselves. The conductor walks in and instead of introducing the pieces, raises his baton until both the audience and the orchestra are quiet and attentive.

The first piece by Wagner, a Siegfried Idyll, has some of the rising violin arpeggios characteristic of his great operatic works but it is restrained. It is clearly about romantic love. "What do you feel about that Wagnerian bit?" he asks. "Nice," one of them remarks, but does not go any further.

The conductor turns to the audience. "That piece of music was a birthday present to the composer's wife. He gathered an ensemble at six in the morning to awaken her. Nice way to be woken up on your birthday," he says.

Next our violinist is introduced. Although our young Fremantle orchestra are talented and play well together, both they, and the audience are in awe of this soloist. He is of international standing.

He leads the orchestra through a medley of light and tuneful pieces of Tchaikovsky grouped under the name 'Un Chere Lieu' (A Dear Place), which delights the audience. After 3 rounds of applause he returns to acknowledge the audience's wish for him to play something else.

He readies himself again, the violin body fitting neatly under his chin, his left hand fingers curling over the strings in readiness, his feet a foot apart. "Bach's Second Sonata in A minor, Andante". He seems almost to bark it out.

Within 2 bars our doctor is shaking, as great sobs come welling up from within his chest, and tears flow unrestrained down his cheeks. It is as if all the suffering in the world is contained within this music - all the mothers who have lost their sons in useless wars, all the people on the street who have lost all hope for a better day and faith their suffering has some meaning. He wonders how the violinist can go on playing. He glances furtively at the audience. They are just quiet and give a dutiful applause at the end of the piece. He turns to his grandchildren and asks them what they think. By now he has wiped his cheeks. "That was really sad Granddad", the youngest replies.

Next morning he is wondering why and how all this happened to him? Come on, it was a just a piece of music! He goes to You Tube, to find the piece played by different violinists. He wants to know whether it has the same effect on him, as it did the previous afternoon. No, it is clearly an often played classic piece and it in no way touches him as it did the previous day.

Three days later, he attends a Freo Street Doctor clinic. He learns that one of his patients, a man who was easy to engage with, and had talent as an artist, had taken his life. Both he and his colleagues are sad and shaken. He sits and reflects. Why is he engaging in this work when it all seems useless, almost thrown back in his face? What to do about this lump of sadness settling in his solar plexus? Then suddenly comes these words, floating into his mind.

"No man is an island entire of itself … When one man dies one chapter is not torn out of the book, but translated into a better language and every chapter must be so translated … Therefore never send to know for whom the bell tolls, it tolls for thee."

Humbling words of John Donne from 400 years ago, who lived in a more religious and enquiring age. These words are as true now as they were then.

The Ravens' Requiem for a Tree

There is, or was, a eucalyptus tree in our neighbour's garden. It rises almost 30 metres to the sky - the tallest tree for miles around. There is a certain magnificence to this tree connecting earth to sky and the sky to the earth.

It is said that a tree this size raises about a thousand litres of water a day to be transpired through its leaves which in turn convert the carbon dioxide of the air with the water to make eucalyptus oil, amongst many other products. I guess its age may be similar to my own, about eighty years. It was probably planted by the first owner.

We have watched many times its smooth white bark reflect a pinkish golden glow from the rays of the setting sun. What draws our admiration and wonder is the way it defies gravity with its subtle strength which enables it to have such a fine and delicate posture. Its branches ascend into more and more fine divisions and then to an abundance of foliage. It has resisted so many fierce winds that have passed our way.

It is, of course, the home of many birds, chief of whom are the ravens. They fly up into its mid to upper branches and from there call to their mates perched in the trees in our garden. A study has been made of raven calls and up to 70 different sequences have been found. They mate for life and are very social birds. I did not like their harsh calls when I first came to Western Australia. I longed for the sweet songs of a blackbird of my youth in Sussex. Now, my body, my senses, and my ears are in tune with the vibrations and emanations of Mother Nature here, in this part of our beloved Gaia. I watch how different species of birds seem to dominate the garden at any time in the change of seasons. Magpies may chase off the ravens and vice versa, while both may be told to go away by a tiny Willy Wagtail.

For a long time this tree which we loved was feared by another neighbour, whose house lies closer to it. He has wanted it chopped down for quite some time. Quite recently, the owners of the tree, saw a large branch fall and when the neighbour once again approached them about the tree, they agreed to end its life. They were going away and wanted all risks out of the way.

Four days ago the tree loppers came and the air was filled with the high whine of the chain saw and the heavy grinding sound of the wood mulcher. It was distressing. Three quarters of the branches were lopped and we saw what a dangerous job this was, where each branch had to be tied and lowered, while the tree surgeon secured himself to the tree. The following day it was windy so work ceased.

Yesterday morning I heard a sound I had never heard before. Over a hundred ravens had gathered from far and near. They were cawing and at the same time flying in a circle around the tree. They were definitely saying something as the sounds were many and varied. It sounded as if they were mourning the loss of this tree which had been a communal home and meeting place for so long.

It was truly awe inspiring. It went on for at least half an hour. I asked myself, what are they saying? Are they protesting the failure of us humans to recognise their habitat? Are they mourning the imminent loss of their fellow creature, this magnificent tree which they and their forbears have perched in for almost a century?

Whatever it was, I knew I was witness to an awesome event, in the true meaning of the word.

A Special Place - Suka Mulia

It is situated in the mountains of Sunda half way between Jakarta and Bandung. You reach it by turning off the main road between these two cities just before you get to the mountain resort town of Cipanas, where once we had a holiday cottage on the slopes of Gunung Gede.

Now one has to pass a lot of holiday houses before you get to the real Sundanese country side, which we so loved, where rice paddies mingle with fields of vegetables. Everywhere you can hear the sound of running water, and everywhere there are two or three people on motor bikes or others crammed into tiny buses making their way over the bumpy road, which eventually leads to Suka Mulia. I once rode my horse from Cipanas to this place, which now no-one could do, with all this busy traffic.

It was over fifty years ago when I first visited Suka Mulia, all was country life then, with very little pretence of country living by city people. A very bumpy jeep ride led us to the gates of the property with pine trees on either side. A Wayang was performed that night for friends and locals to celebrate the purchase of the farm. Later the farm was stocked with cows as milk was quite a rarity in Java, but as competition grew with development in the 1970's, it eventually closed down.

Now it is the cemetery for the family of Bapak, and also for friends who came from around the world to be with him in the sixties and seventies. Bapak's body was disinterred twenty years after his death and reburied on the highest piece of land on the property. After all those years in the ground, his body had not decomposed.

At the time of our 2017 visit, we found ourselves in countryside for only the last 3 kilometres of the journey. The pine trees were still growing on either side of the gates. We are driven along through well-trimmed tea bushes on either side, with a steep slope on our left topped by tall trees, until we arrive at the car park.

From there, there are some red tiled steps that rise to a long, bricked path lined by tall palms. Through the trees can be seen Gunung Gede (Mount Gede) twelve kilometres away, reaching to the sky. A small cloud was floating over its summit. In the past, in our cottage on its slopes, we used to occasionally hear the shutters shake at night as Gunung Gede's volcanic base was moved by subterranean forces. Today, even though I can hear the sound of bird calls and the sighing of a soft breeze, there is a silence within me that is so overwhelming it leaves no room for thoughts or feelings.

At the end of the path we climb the two set of steps that lead to the family graveyard. In the middle of it is an enclosed Pendopo with the graves of Bapak and his immediate family around him, while those of his children and their spouses lie in designated areas around. I stand in front of the new grave of Muti, who has just died. No words of prayer come, the Silence and Peace in me is so overwhelming that I have no wish to think or form a prayer. The peaceful silence within is sufficient.

We return to the car park and drive a short distance to the new cemetery made for friends of the family both Indonesian and expatriate. There is a delightful light filled room where we can sit and have our breakfast. We are hungry as we left Jakarta at four in the morning.

There are two rows of graves, all of oblong raised grey marble with simply the name of the person, their birth and death date. We have known almost all of them. There are no irrelevant sentimental sayings like 'Always in our hearts'. Such nonsense seems to me to mock the reality of eternity.

We have bought two places here to be buried in but I now realise that this life moves forward, not backward, and paradoxically the wish to be buried here has moved on, as has my life. The past is the past and the future is the indeterminate future, the Now is the eternal Now.

Finding My Father's Grave

It is 1993 and I am on a night train from Chennai to Salem where my father lies buried with Ravichandran, who has done so much to arrange this journey. As the wheels of the train rumble and rock rhythmically under us, I ask him why he had joined the spiritual way of Subud. "To be able to face the difficulties in my life", he answers. Ravi is a high caste Brahmin and works as a petrol station attendant. He, his wife, his mother, and brother and sister-in-law all live in a house the size of my sitting room. The floor is of mud, polished with cow dung. I ask about the principles and practice of Hinduism. We share our ideas and experiences of life. His deep brown eyes radiate warmth, kindness, and caring. For the second time in my life I feel I have found another brother - yes another brown brother. In fact, his letters to me are addressed 'Dear Brother Rachman'.

My father died in April 1947 in India, four months before Independence. I was twelve, and I silently grieved for ten years, until I had an Inner experience that healed me. In the mid 1970's the wish arose in me to search for his grave while living in the Subud compound in Cilandak.

At the end of Ramadan it is customary in Indonesia to ask one another and especially one's parents for forgiveness for the words or actions that may have hurt them. It is also the custom to visit the graves of relatives at this time.

So, this is the reason for the arising of the wish for me to find my father's grave. I had no idea where he was buried. All I had was a photo. I asked the Embassy in Jakarta, where I worked, to make enquiries. A month later I had a letter from the British High Commission in India enclosing a letter from Mr Bhoja Bhatty, Head of the Forestry Department of the Republic of India. He said that he had been the assistant to my father when he died and that he was buried in Salem in Tamil Nadu. He gave me a warm invitation to meet him should I come. A map of the cemetery was enclosed.

The following day an Indian visitor came to my clinic with a note from his doctor to give him an injection of B12. As I was withdrawing the needle from his buttock, I asked him where Salem was. "That's strange. That is my home town", he said. "Come and stay with me and I will take you to your father's grave". Time and circumstance caught up with me and it was not possible to follow up on this generous offer. It was not until 1989 that I met Ravi, Ashwin and Mansur Sultan in Sydney at a Subud Congress. They immediately said they would arrange the visit.

So back to my train journey to Salem. We arrive as a red dawn is breaking. The sound of the crows and the minah birds are echoing in our ears. I feel as if I am back in time to 42 years ago, although I have never been here before. The Forestry Office smells of camphor and I learn that my father had written a small treatise, which is still used for that particular timber.

Mr Bhatty is waiting for us, with breakfast ready at the visitor's bungalow. He has been brought all the way from Bangalore by another set of Indian friends. He is a tall Karnataka man with a military bearing. He is now retired but is Chair of the Wild Life Fund for India.

He looks me in the eye and says he can see my father in me. He describes how my father had prepared him for his forestry exams and passed him. "Not really tough enough on me", he says.

I did not realise my father had reached the top of his profession as a Conservator of Forests, with an area the size of Wales to look after, and that he had been invited to stay on by the Indian Government-in-waiting. After breakfast we make our way to the cemetery, entering between two little wooden kiosks beside the road, past some pigs rooting in the ground.

This cemetery is where the British from 200 years of the Raj have been laid to rest, some with enormous blocks of stone to commemorate their lives. The words of grief and sadness engraved on these stones of those who have died far from their homeland are now only witnessed by the sun, the wind, the rain and the long unkempt grass. That is all except my father's grave, which is now newly whitewashed, with garlands of flowers around the granite headstone, cleaned as if new with the words Commander JEM Mitchell beloved husband of May (my stepmother). He had not wanted to live to an old age and his wish had been granted to him.

Two forest officers stand at attention by the side of the grave and I almost expect them to salute. I am not sure why I am choking with emotion. The grief has long gone but I am aware this is a ceremony to honour both my father and the forestry service, in which he served. It is now part of the Government of the Republic of India and no longer part of the British Empire. The honour bestowed on my father and myself, illustrated this change.

We go on to see the house where my father lived. It is now a girl's school with fifty desks in each room. The upper veranda looks out over the Nilgri hills in the distance. There is a white wall around the eight acre grounds.

I view the stairs where he fell, and the red tiles, where his head hit before he died. He had got up in the early hours of the morning after a party when he heard a noise from downstairs. I know now the how, and the where of his death. The why of course alludes me. But I know for certain that he was, and is, a happy soul. He lived by his values of honour, service, love and respect for his fellow human beings, even during the hubris of Empire. The people around respected and loved him enough to ask him to stay on after independence.

The whole episode is written up in the local office files. I am not too insistent on reading them, and Mr Bhatty is glad that I don't press him. I know that a surfeit of whisky may have been a contributing cause. He was a *bon viveur* and enjoyed life to the full. Mr Bhatty explains that the house is run down now. It used to have polished teak wood everywhere. After my father's death, he later lived in it as well.

We wander around town, drink some coconut juice and have a meal. Later in the evening Ravi and I go back together to the grave. As I stand in front of it I am overcome with gratitude for the healing of the grief that I experienced as an adolescent, and for the care and love of my friends, especially my Indian friends, for bringing me here, and for the bountiful Mercy of the Almighty. I am in awe of the extraordinary set of coincidences that have led to my being here.

However, as I look back now I feel that there is no such thing as COINCIDENCE. This is only Kismet, Destiny and the underlying Reality of a Power that enfolds Everything inwardly and outwardly including all of us humans who are connected as One Humanity.

Fourteen years ago Ravi had a sudden headache and was taken to hospital where he died. Many mourned his death including myself. I feel privileged to have known this man who showed such love and care for his fellow human beings.

Street Doctor

It is nice to go to a warm, clean, dry bed at night and wake in the morning, to look through the open French doors of the bedroom at all the greenery in the garden and listen to the sound of the fountain and the chortle of the magpie's song. It is not like that for many of our fellow humans who are homeless and sleep rough in the parks or beaches around us, subject to rain, wind and the assault of others.

My concern for my fellow human beings in this situation, and the wish to do something practical to help, arose in me in my sixties. I noticed how uncomfortable street people were who came to the general practice clinic that I was working in, particularly those suffering various addictions. There are many opinions and judgements on such people, from failure to discipline themselves, to being lazy and so on. I found the view 'down on their luck' suited me more.

I remember one particular elderly man who suffered from chronic schizophrenia. He always wore three overcoats come summer or winter. He relished being free and to sleep anywhere he wanted but realised the time was coming that he would need some care from others.

There was a group of doctors in our division of general practice who decided to be of better service to these kind of patients and bring the clinic to them rather than the other way round. Funding was found to buy a bus fitted out with an examination couch, benches for the patient, doctor and nurse to sit on and cupboards for all the required equipment. It required us to be 'up close and personal' with the patient because of the small size of the space, and for the nurse and doctor to work closely together in an egalitarian and mutually respectful spirit.

It was not easy work, in fact very difficult, as our efforts to facilitate healthier ways of living were so often frustrated by the deeply ingrained habits of addictive behaviour that we all have to some degree. Are we not all on a journey of development which is only possible through the Grace of the Life Force which envelops us all inwardly and outwardly? We can all learn from one another, from the so called 'down and out' to those of us in the medical profession who may think they know what is needed and best for the health of others.

I was lucky to work with colleagues, both doctors and nurses, mostly women of my daughters' age who were passionate about social justice.

Miracles occur all the time and usually we are not present in ourselves to be aware they are happening, but there was one incident I would like to share which I felt was indeed a miracle.

It often rains in Fremantle, Western Australia in the month of May, and darkness begins to fall around five thirty. The Street Doctor bus was parked in a small, grassy square opposite our rather nice railway station built in the optimistic Edwardian era. Douglas firs dripped rain on passers-by. Our shift was from 4 to 7 in the evening. It was warm and cosy in the bus, though rainy, dark and wet outside.

Our first patient was a Vietnamese man who wanted to set fire to himself. The business he had set up after many struggles had collapsed, as he thought, through he betrayal of his business partner. It was a long struggle for my nursing colleague and I to persuade him that life still had something to offer him.

Our next patient was a recovered heroin addict who was in constant pain from a pin in her ankle joint, put there because of a previous fracture. All Emergency Response departments and other GPs had refused painkillers on the basis of her previous drug convictions. She had just got a job as a house painter and had earned two weeks pay but her daughter had dumped her newly-born baby on her. That took a lot of sorting out, with no easy solutions.

As we were preparing to pack up, one of our well-known and frequent patients knocked on the door. She was an indigenous woman who had given birth many times and had been physically abused with resulting fractures to jaw, collar bone, and ribs. She also had Hepatitis C and B and several sexually transmitted diseases. She had suffered more than her fair share of the 'slings and arrows of outrageous fortune' and she began to scream and yell "I have had enough, I HAVE HAD ENOUGH".

The sound of her cries filled the bus and with it the misery and suffering of so much of mankind, the results of man's inhumanity to man. Worse was the realisation of the hopelessness of anything that we could DO to alleviate it. Suddenly amid the noise of her yelling and screaming, I let go and a Silence began to emerge in the centre of me, which I felt my nursing colleague also experiencing. It grew and seemed to encompass the misery and the suffering of this poor but enduring and courageous woman. At last the screaming stopped and we could give her a few words of practical advice.

Next week she returned her face smiling and relaxed. She said to me "Dr Rachman, if you let me, I would like to put my arms around your neck, kiss you and give you a hug".

Another Moment of Truth in my life to be treasured.

Appendix
Family and Ancestors

Emily Coleman - the Mayor of Margate's Daughter

The desire to trace one's ancestry is common across time and cultures. In current times, television shows tracing the family history of celebrities are popular, and companies have sprung up to assist those interested in tracing their predecessors. Some religious groups such as the Mormons regard this as a sacred duty. Certain cultures such as the Yemeni and people from Mali can trace their families back 600 years or more and of course we read in the Bible of men recounting their ancestors. In Islam a Syed is one descended from the family of the Prophet.

Everyone would like to have illustrious ancestors. This sometimes occurs but more often people are confronted by the suffering or lowliness of their forebears.

Through the spiritual training of the Subud latihan, I have become conscious of those tendencies in me which prevent me from being the kind of person who is capable of real understanding and compassion in both my behaviour and my awareness. I am also aware of those strivings that lie deep within me to comprehend the meaning of life. These stirrings came early in life, before I could be said to be influenced by the thought of others. I dimly intuit these tendencies were handed down in my "genes".

For all these reasons, I have an interest in tracing my ancestors, and had an opportunity to do this when visiting England some years ago.

We were house-sitting for Sachlan, our youngest son, who lives near London when I spied a trowel that lay in a cupboard alongside some plates and dishes. This trowel, with an ivory handle and silver engraving on it, had lain on my parent's hall table for over forty years. I think my mother felt some pride in it as one of her ancestors had been in a 'position' in society. She was socially class conscious and yet disliked snobbery.

The engraving stated that the Mayor of Margate, Joseph Coleman, had used this trowel in laying the foundation stone of a Wesleyan school in Hawley Square in Margate in 1896. I knew my maternal grandmother was born Emily Coleman and presumed this must have been her father, my mother's grandfather. I decided to Google the Mayors of Margate and indeed found Joseph Coleman was Mayor at that time.

I made contact with a local historian, who had some photos of the Mayor Joseph Coleman and his wife Selina. Rohana and I decided to do a trip down to Margate to find Hawley Square. It was a cold and cloudy day but we found the square which had been built by a Sir Henry Hawley 'for the local nobility and gentry' in the mid-1700s. Lovely Queen Anne type houses surrounded the large grass-lawned square. The school had the name of my great grandfather engraved on a plaque as the founder of the school. Next-door was the Wesleyan Chapel, which I later found was where my grandparents Samuel Lawrie and Emily Coleman were married in 1902.

At the corner of the square is a theatre, small but still running, the second oldest in Britain. There is a notice in the square saying that the Wesley brothers had preached there and that John Keats had also visited. Clearly there had been some culture in this town in the past. It was said that Emily had done quite a bit of travelling and had gone to China amongst other places. However she leaves no notes about her life.

Impressions about her from my sister are somewhat negative. Norah, our mother, married at nineteen to get away from Emily. She seemed to wear the pants in the Lawrie household in Crawford Road Edinburgh, and dominated our sweet-natured grandfather

Samuel. She sacked a servant for stealing. My sister Roanna had therefore thrown away the picture of her that always stood on my mother's dressing table. A great pity.

However, Emily's letters to my mother Norah certainly show a lot of caring. Manners were different in those days, according to society's norms. I remember Emily as a woman of style with an enquiring look on her face.

The local historian sent me a photo of Joseph and Selina and a photo of the gravestone of the Lawrie family. This included Robert Lawrie, my grandfather's youngest brother, who was killed in 1918 in General Allenby's attack on Jerusalem. There he is buried. Obviously there was a lot of sorrow in the family over his death. I was named after him, Robert. Perhaps this is one of the reasons I have always been interested in Jerusalem. This is also the place where Jesus and Mohammed had their Ascensions. The words and example of both these prophets have touched my life. But there is this additional family linkage which may too have spurred my sense of connection with Jerusalem.

So threads of meaning pass down through families.

Finding My Maternal Grandfather Samuel Lawrie

Serendipity means finding something interesting while proceeding along another path. It also means by chance, destiny, karma and kismet. Synchronicity is when events happen which coincide and seem to have a special meaning. Perhaps my meeting with Richard and Marie Phillips would be described by neither of these terms but simply by the words of my religious maternal grandfather as Providence.

Possibly in my case it all means the same. Something happens which begins to give an answer to a long unanswered question going back to early youth, and for the most part forgotten in the duties and responsibilities of adulthood. The question was "Where do I come from?"

This question has many layers, but one is very simple. Where did my parents come from? What was the place like where they were brought up, its particular culture and background? What were the life questions that they asked themselves and perhaps pondered on? In particular what was my maternal grandfather Samuel Lawrie like? His work and efforts initially supported his sister and parents, and continued to support his children and grandchildren long after his death. I knew he ran a business in Princes Street Edinburgh but he had always wanted to be a minister of the church.

One particularly providential event happened during a holiday in Scotland at the age of twelve. It happened within a few metres of his shop, just two days before the news reached me of my father's death. An old lady passing by accosted me and said, "Whatever happens to you, trust in the Lord". That was something I was unable to do at that time but whose meaning was to gradually unfold in my life, and which indeed continues to do so.

The opportunity to explore the question 'Where do I come from?' came when I was in Yemen in the 1980's and met the Philips at the British Embassy club where many of us gathered on Fridays to play tennis and be social.

Marie Philip ran a Highland dancing group every fortnight and we soon formed a friendship with Marie and Richard and their children. Sometime after leaving Yemen, when visiting Scotland, we came to stayed at their home in Edinburgh. This just 'chanced' to be a hundred metres or so from where my maternal grandparents had lived in Crawford Road. It was here my mother and my aunts had spent their childhood and youth. They sang in the amateur operatic society of Edinburgh and Edith, my youngest aunt, had taken leading roles.

It was also by chance that the Phillip's house was in the same style as my grandparent's. Beautiful large Georgian style windows let in lots of light and there were two main sitting rooms, one above the other, with the grand piano in the upper room.

I was only six months old when my mother took me from India to see her parents in their house. It had black and white tiles on the ground floor, a feature I have always liked and which we had in one of our houses. My sister told me that Sunday was the time for the family to gather for a meal and then afterwards to go upstairs to sing together.

I have a letter, which is warm and consoling, from my great grandmother Isobel Lawrie to my mother, Norah Isobel, when she lost her first son Jackie to diphtheria. My mother had just gone out to India and was only 20 years old. My great grandmother's maiden name was Isobel Thompson and she was also from Kent. My mother once told me how much she appreciated this grandmother who brought some real feeling into the somewhat dour Scottish atmosphere of her family.

I mentioned that St George's had been the church where my grandfather Samuel Lawrie was an elder. The Minister James Black had been his great friend and it was said that Samuel had his heart attack while visiting the Reverent Black and died in his arms. A nice subject for a romantic Victorian painting!

I visited St George's during the Edinburgh Festival. The big hall before entering the church proper was a hive of activity. The Soweto Choir were about to sing there that evening and all tickets were sold. The Church was not of the usual type with a long aisle but rather shaped in a circle. Upstairs there was another hall, almost empty, with paintings illustrating the Rubayat of Omar Khayyam, a favourite of mine as a young man. I could not go into the church itself unless I bought a ticket for the enactment of St Matthew's Gospel.

Wow what a revolutionary text this is! The standards to be a true Christian are so high that no wonder the Lord's Prayer should be said 50 times a day. I wondered how my grandfather felt sitting there on a Sunday some eighty years ago with his three daughters beside him. My mother had told me that he did nod off in the sermons occasionally until the minister would strike the pulpit with some quotation from the Bible that had "Wake up" in it.

On walking out of the church I noticed a large black plaque on the wall to my left. It was in memory to the Reverent James Black who had been chaplain to King George the Sixth and minister of that church. His sermons and writing are still read.

As I traced my steps back along Princes Street with the shops beneath the tall Georgian styled buildings on the left of me and the castle up on the great rocky hill to the right I thought about Samuel Lawrie and felt gratitude for his care and sacrifices which had reached down and benefited me.

Two years later I revisited Scotland, this time to take my sister Roanna who is 8 years older than me. We were invited to stay with the Philips and this time Marie contacted the owners of the house my grandparents had lived in, and an invitation was given to see around the old home of our grandparents. Roanna who had stayed there was thrilled. She could remember every room and the memories of childhood came flooding back. What I sensed most was the feeling of community going back generations which is the better side of Edinburgh. This feeling of friendship is really important. It is brought out in the books of Alexander McCall Smith who lives in the town and writes so affectionately of it.

I have only done a little research on births, marriage and deaths of my two maternal grandparents. How much of their life story lies simply buried in the memories of those who have already 'passed on'? Does it matter?

Well, in a way it does. Each of us needs to become aware of our own identity, and much of it is what we have inherited both genetically and socially. It is only in becoming free of the mistakes of our ancestors that we can become free ourselves, and be of real benefit to those who have gone before us.

My Paternal Grandmother Mary Anne Mitchell

I feel it is important to know about my grandparents because they are in my blood and bones, my essence.

I inherited a snobbish attitude, as if somehow my family is of upper class stock. As I take up the genealogy search, I find that nothing could be further from the truth. I find words like, labourer, mariner, domestic servant, table maid, written down as my forbears 'profession'. My paternal grandfather is written down in my parents' marriage certificate as Captain, RN while on his death certificate it is Chief Officer in other words Chief Petty Officer, a non-commissioned officer. It is my father who rises to the rank of an officer, Commander J.E.M. Mitchell. This is mainly because his father sent him to Dartmouth Naval College, where he graduated as a midshipman and soon took his Lieutenant's exam and passed. Hence his fellow lieutenants are present in his wedding photograph.

I see from the birth certificates and censuses that Mary Anne was born illegitimate in 1861. In the census held that year she is two weeks old, with the name of Mary Anne Wilson, the name of her biological father. The other two members of the household are her grandmother Mary Pride, aged 63, and her mother Elizabeth Pride aged 25.

At the next census ten years later, she is Mary Anne Pride and is recorded as the daughter of James Pride. Elizabeth and he had married 4 years earlier and now have a son, James, and a 2-month old daughter, Elizabeth. Mary Anne is for a brief moment in a family, aged 10 and recognised as the daughter of James Pride. In the next census in 1881 she is a table maid, in a 'downstairs' position in a large house with many servants in St George's Square. In the 1891 census, she is a general domestic servant in a house of mostly older people and it is difficult to know who the other servants are and who are the owners.

In 1886 she is married to John Mitchell, Chief Officer who is 22 years older than her. On the marriage certificate she calls herself Mary Anne Wilson again, with her father listed as William Wilson, deceased, profession printer. Her identity is therefore somewhat split. In the marriage certificate of her son, John Ebenezer Miller Mitchell, her maiden name is mentioned as Miller. So where are we? Pride, Miller or Wilson?

My feeling is that her life was a struggle. There was much hard work and serving others who were her 'betters'. Was she respected enough? Was she honoured enough as a daughter, a sister and above all, as a mother and grandmother?

These are questions in my heart, even as I reflect the defects in my own relationship with my mother, especially not being present at her death, which I very much regret. My father was not present at his mother Mary Anne's death. Perhaps he was caught up in the preparations for war, as I was caught up in attending to Bapak.

What are the essentials of human life? "Honour thy mother and thy father all the days of thy life." How surprised I am to hear this old Scottish Presbyterian Covenanter now talking through me.

But it is true. Honour and respect are part of the love that a child owes his or her parents, whatever the faults in their character. This should come first in the centre of our Being.

So Mary Anne, I would not be here writing this now, but for you. You are part of my inheritance. The quiet, the retired and simple person that you were, so proud of your son who was making his way in the world, in a way that was never possible for you.

I, your grandson, who saw you only once, honour you, my Grandmother Mary Anne. I have lived many more years than your son, my father, and have had enough time and suffering to know the value of being simple and not assuming airs and graces.

My Sailor Grandfather

My paternal grandfather, John Mitchell, died fifteen years before I was born in 1934. He was born in 1845.

My father spoke of him with great pride the day we met together for the last time, before he departed for India in 1946. He had just been demobilised from the Royal Navy.

He told me at the age of 15 his father "ran away" to sea to escape going into the Church. For three years he sailed in those great, three masted schooners like the Cutty Sark, which now lies at Greenwich. They raced from Shanghai to London to bring their cargo of tea to eager buyers, for the first to get there, got the best price.

He spoke of the rigours of the sea, with four hour watches, sleeping below decks in hammocks just 14 inches wide. The clambering up the rigging in a storm to change the mizzen sails, with feet on slippery cross masts or rope, and a hundred foot drop to the deck.

Did the great Windjammers sometimes get becalmed before entering into the Roaring Forties, and did John contemplate the great panoply of the Night Sky reflected in the mirror of a still ocean?

It was clearly a culture that disappeared with the advent of steam. What now seems clear is it was an education in itself. From the perusal of death and birth certificates I discovered from the National Registry Office in Edinburgh, my great grandfather Ebenezer Mitchell died when my grandfather was fifteen. The likelihood was that the family were too poor to send him to a good school, so joining the merchant fleet for training as a sailor was an alternative to going to school.

My father spoke of John returning from one of the voyages with his friend Saville, a member of the family that ran the famous Shaw Saville shipping line. His friend was met by a coach, my grandfather had to walk the wet, cobbled streets back to his home in Leith.

John joined the Royal Navy at the age of 18 and continued with his training as a sailor, eventually ending up as a captain. My father showed me a photo of a tall man in naval uniform with a beard looking rather severe. I was also told that he was a friend of Colonel Baden Powell, who asked him to set up the first Sea Scout group. Discipline was strict and 'the rope's end' administered if required.

Deciphering myth from fact is always difficult but death certificates probably do not lie. Under the heading of 'Profession' on his death certificate is filled in, "First Officer" and "Gunnery Officer". I think this means that he never took the Lieutenant's exam that would have made him a commissioned officer.

John took great pains to see that my father was sent to Dartmouth College, where candidates for naval officers received an excellent tertiary education. My father ended up as a Commander RN. He was very proud of that achievement and that title.

Perusal of the death and marriage certificates revealed something else I had not known before. John had married twice. When his first wife Marie King died, he married my grandmother, Mary Anne, in 1892 when he was already forty-seven years old. Again looking at birth certificates they reveal that he had a sister Jane, born two years after him, and two sisters older than him, Margaret and Isabella.

I have always loved the sea in all its moods. Is there anything in our family now which can lay claim to the experiences of John? He sought independence, self-reliance, maybe mate-ship through signing up as a crew member of those Cutty Sark-like ships that raced from Shanghai to London, 150 years ago. Was his appetite for risk and adventure passed down to his descendants?

Like John, I have been incredibly lucky in the opportunities that arose during my life, including the education I had. This was paid for by my parents, and by the English Speaking Union scholarship that gave me a year at a top school in the US. I studied hard as I had ambition to do well. I was fortunate to live as a student at Coombe Springs, where people seeking Meaning in their lives worked on themselves to find out how to wake up and really live a whole life. 'The Work' allowed someone like myself, who is somewhat lazy by nature, to experience the value of work. It was not until later, however, that I discovered what I truly liked doing was applying my intelligence to helping people. It was doing that which gave me a deep feeling of satisfaction.

The greatest good fortune which happened in my life, was to receive the Subud latihan and to be close to Bapak, the person who first received it. There in front of me was proof that Human Compassion and Wisdom could, and did, exist. We had this experience because Rohana and I were lucky enough to be able to live in Wisma Subud

Where are the influences that can arouse the sense and meaning of a person's life? How and where can they find the means to wake up to the joy and happiness of Life?

I observe the lives of my children and grandchildren with interest. I hope the spirit of John emerges in future generations of our family, and that some descendants will explore the possibilities of life with the courage and adventurous spirit of their ancestor, John Mitchell.

I also hope that my account of finding the latihan and living a life guided by it will interest my descendants, and perhaps other seekers.

It has healed, inspired and sustained me and has brought me closer to God. The latihan is for all humanity. My life has been guided and immensely enriched by it and stories from my journey are what I want to leave for others. I do so in the hope readers may find out the value and truth of this path for themselves.

Glossary

Bapak: Indonesian word for father or respected older man. In this book it refers to Muhammad Subuh Sumohadiwidjojo, also known as Pak Subuh.

Cilandak: Once an isolated village south of Jakarta and now a busy crowded suburb of that city.

Helper: An experienced Subud member who has been authorised to pass on the latihan to new members.

Ibu: Indonesian word for mother or respected older woman.

Latihan kejiwaan: Indonesian word meaning spiritual exercise or training, usually abbreviated to latihan.

Opening: the first time a person attends the latihan in the presence of Helpers.

Pendopo: An open hall or patio for receiving guests in front of a Javanese house.

Ramadan: Islamic holy month of fasting.

Receiving: The guidance and experiences that arise within oneself as a result of the latihan.

Selamatan: Ceremonial meal or feast, following prayers, to celebrate or commemorate a rite of passage or other significant occasion in life.

Souk: An Arab market place.

Subud: A contraction of the Javanese words Susila Budhi Dharma, encompassing the meaning of all three of those words:
> *Susila*: Humane.
> *Budhi*: Because of God
> *Dharma:* Through surrender to God

Also refers to the organisation, a spiritual movement first registered in Indonesia in 1949, and now legally known internationally as The World Subud Association.

Subuh: Indonesian word meaning dawn and having no direct connection with the word Subud. Bapak was given this name because he was born at dawn.

Suka Mulia: A place in the hills near to Jakarta originally used as a farming enterprise. Now the site of Bapak's grave, his family and those who chose to live near him.

Test, testing: This has a special meaning in Subud. It means a method of finding answers, through the latihan by the Grace of God.

Wisma: Literally 'house of' or 'home of', applied to a large building or compound of houses belonging to a specific owner or groups e.g. Wisma Subud.

Zikr, zikir: Usually means devotional acts in Islam in which prayers are repeatedly recited silently within the mind or aloud. In this book it means the experience of a certain beat or rhythm that can arise within one.

Books to read

For an introduction to Subud:

A Reporter In Subud - Varindra Tarzie Vittachi

A Life Within A Life: An Introduction To Subud - Dominic Rieu

Concerning Subud - John Godolphin Bennett

History of Subud Volume 1 - Harlinah Longcroft

Biographies of other Subud people:

Autobiography - Muhammad Subuh Sumohadiwidjojo

Beyond the Breakers: A Subud Odyssey - Silvana Waniuk

Reminiscences of Bapak and of My Life - Arthur Abdullah Pope

Antidote, Experience of a Spiritual Energy – Salamah Pope

Subud - A Spiritual Journey - Rozak Tatebe

The Path of Subud - Husein Rofe

A Life in Subud - Raymond Van Sommers

The Dawning: A Grace Untold - Emmanuel Eliot

My Stairway to Subud - Anthony Bright-Paul

Source of Light – Leonard Lassalle

Saving Grace – Marcus Bolt

If you would like further information about Subud and its activities please go to www.subud.com and follow the link 'What is Subud?'

Printed in the United States
By Bookmasters